# a little bit of
# meditation

# a little bit of
# meditation

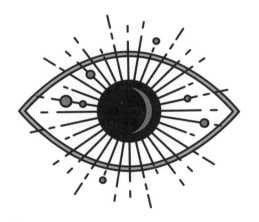

## an introduction to
## focus

## AMY LEIGH MERCREE

STERLING ETHOS
New York

STERLING ETHOS
New York

STERLING ETHOS and the distinctive Sterling Ethos logo
are registered trademarks of Sterling Publishing Co., Inc.

Text © 2017 Amy Leigh Mercree

ISBN 978-1-4549-2689-4
ISBN 978-1-4549-2690-0 (e-book)

For information about custom editions, special sales, and premium
purchases, please contact specialsales@unionsquareandco.com.

Printed in India

10 12 14 16 18 17 15 13 11 9

unionsquareandco.com

Cover and interior design by Melissa Farris
Cover and interior illustration by Marish/Shutterstock.com

# contents

# INTRODUCTION

Nowadays in our culture, many roads lead to the art and cultivation of mindfulness. When people seek treatment for anxiety, oftentimes meditation is recommended. When people seek to learn meditation, mindfulness is a result. It is not a new idea that, if we are conscious to and present in the moment we are experiencing at the exclusion of almost everything else, we will be more happy and healthy. Meditation has been used in Eastern religions since ancient times.

The idea of consciousness has been gaining popularity since the 1960s in the Western world. Consciousness is the infinite awareness of being within us all. It is the witnessing part of the self always in the background observing life around you. Meditation, in its many forms, cultivates awareness of consciousness.

In *A Little Bit of Meditation,* we will explore the history of the practice of meditation and its origins, as well as learn practical applications of how to bring conscious awareness into daily life to improve the quality of our experience on Earth. We will discuss the physical, emotional, mental, and spiritual ramifications of meditating in daily life. A wide variety of practical activities and meditations are included in this volume. So dive in and find your center!

# 1
# the history of meditation

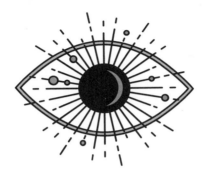

*Meditation* and *mindfulness* have become trendy buzzwords in pop culture over the last decade. Meditation practices are no longer relegated to trained practitioners who live in monasteries or ashrams, or adherents to exotic religions and mystical groups. These days, meditation has become a practice that is accessible to almost everyone. It is no longer simply a spiritual tool, either; it has been quickly garnering the backing of neuroscience and other medical specialties because of the health benefits it supplies.

What has sparked the upsurge of interest in meditation? It is thought to have existed for many thousands of years, so why the sudden popularity among diverse groups of people? One answer is the simple fact that the scientific community is giving it credence as a reliable method of stress relief and tool to deal with things such as trauma. Some people believe that the rapidly growing popularity is also due to evolution of consciousness among humanity. Finally, in a world that is increasingly chaotic and moving at a frantic pace, people are seeking out ways to implement calmness and balance in their lives.

## MEDITATION IN ANTIQUITY

The earliest known teachings on meditation came from ancient Hindu religious forms, circa 1500 BCE, from the Vedic texts. This practice of dhyana translates roughly from Sanskrit as contemplation or reflection, and refers to nonjudgmental awareness and sustained attention. This concept was further developed centuries later in Buddhism, Jainism, and formal Hinduism, albeit with slightly different understandings of what it meant.

The internal urge to live a mindful life is not new. In fact, the idea of being present 100 percent of the time has been desirable to some people for thousands of years. Ancient peoples recognized that focusing on one thing at a time could increase productivity and also result in a more pleasurable life.

They worked to cultivate systems and protocols that increase the mind's ability to focus. Aspects of meditation were geared in this direction. In antiquity, this work combined with religious devotion to produce calm, focus, and connection to something larger than one's self.

Meditation can be a doorway to mindfulness. It's interesting how the world's different religions and cultures look to processes of quieting and stilling the mind, and thereby do everything from foster a religious connection to find peace amid stress. These endeavors signify evolution, humanity, and a revolution in understanding consciousness.

## Early Meditation in Major Faith Traditions

Some form of meditation exists in almost every major faith tradition. These largely arose out of the spread of ideas throughout antiquity and increased with broadening travel and trade during the Middle Ages. As groups of people began expanding outward more from their cultural centers, they took their spiritual practices with them. Many scholars believe that meditation practices first appeared in early Vedic teachings, and then developed further in other Asian traditions such as Confucianism, Taoism, and Buddhism.

Meditation forms were present in more than just the major religions of the world. Native American and other indigenous groups had numerous contemplative, meditative, and devotional practices.

## Hinduism

Meditation in Hinduism developed out of early Vedic texts, and later, the Upanishads. The earliest forms of meditation were focused on trying to understand ultimate reality. Is the universe a projection of humanity, or is humanity a projection of the universe? Is the universe an illusion, or is our individual existence an illusion?

Scholars of early Hinduism are aware of four types of meditation based on the ancient texts. Rishis were ancient seers or sages who took what they learned from meditation and composed hymns about their conclusions. They wrote of mantra meditation, visual meditation, meditation on learned insights in the heart and mind, and, finally, an ecstatic state that occurs when merging with the universal reality of Brahman (divinity). Early Hinduism also had ascetic adherents who incorporated various other practices such as breath control and the ability to levitate. Similar descriptions of ascetic shaman-seers have been included in modern-day writings like *Autobiography of a Yogi* by Paramahansa Yogananda.

Hindu meditation developed over the centuries as a multifaceted approach to self-realization called Yoga Vedanta. The yogic path includes components such as service, knowledge, and devotion, and is variable according to each individual's needs. Because Hinduism dates back thousands of years, many schools of thought have risen from it with nuanced differences in belief and practice.

## Buddhism

Buddhism developed in India out of early Hinduism. Unlike the yogic eight-limb path—eight guidelines to living a meaningful and purposeful life as outlined by the sage Patanjali—Buddhism emphasizes three "trainings." Many Americans are most familiar with just the meditation training. However, the other two trainings, wisdom and ethics, are considered to be interconnected with the practice of meditation. Following the death of the Buddha, several doctrinal canons emerged with his supposed teachings. There remains scholarly debate on the authenticity of various portions of these canons, which helped give rise to the different schools of Buddhism.

With the Silk Road—an ancient network of routes that connected distant regions of the Asian continent—opening up trade during the Middle Ages, Buddhist meditation teachings were transmitted out of India and throughout Eastern Asia. Around the eighth century, they spread to Japan in the form of Zen. The primary schools of Buddhism that were cemented over time are Mahayana, Theravada, Pure Land, Zen, and Vajrayana. Each school developed its own meditation practices.

## Judaism

A current of meditation practices has run through Judaism for centuries. As one writer put it, meditation is so wrapped up in the daily rituals of Jewish life that they weren't separated out as individual practices. However, the rituals gave many moments for "meditative awareness," even if they weren't specifically called meditation.

Many of the more technical types of Jewish meditation were recorded as oral traditions, especially in the mystical Kabbalah literature, so they may not have permeated out to the mainstream Jewish population. However, there were many Hebrew words that would have been familiar to lay practitioners that implicitly described various forms of meditation practices such as seclusion, focused concentration, and visualization.

## Christianity

Early Christianity is known for its Desert Fathers and Mothers, ascetics and monks who went out into the wilderness to seclude themselves and commune with God. Early Common Era writings from some of these ascetics point to the practice of mantra meditation, calling it "pure prayer." In the Middle Ages following the East-West Schism in Christianity, the practices of Lectio Divina (a meditative reading of Scripture) and hesychasm (a meditation based on repetition of the Jesus Prayer) developed and took root. Over the centuries, meditative practices remained within various contemplative branches of Christianity, especially within monastic communities. However, they are experiencing a resurgence of popularity within the mainstream Christian population.

## Islam

The bulk of meditation practices in early Islam came through the mystical branch of Sufism. Two early forms, practiced as early as the fourth century AD, were silent dhikr (rhythmic repetition of God's names and attributes) and the meditation of the heart. The motivation behind both of these practices is the intense energy of love, both toward others and toward God. By focusing on love, thoughts and emotions will fade away.

Sufis are most known for the meditative practice of "whirling." Sufi orders were first established in the twelfth century, and many took part in this activity. Whirling is a physical meditation that helps one connect with God through music, movement, and the relinquishment of ego and individual desires. Though whirling is most identified with Sufism, there are several other orders of Sufism and meditation practices as well. One order, started in the fourteenth century, is called the Silent Sufis. They believe that God must be reached only in silence.

# 2

# modern-day religious meditation styles

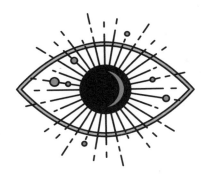

Just as there are countless forms of spiritual thought and practice in our current era, so are there numerous types and nuances of meditation. Some types are an exploration of the true nature of consciousness. Other types of meditation are intended to boost health and fitness. There are versions of meditation that are used to improve cognitive function and help us think better and be more productive. Some people use specific meditation styles to reach a level of peak performance in their profession. Some people see meditation as a spiritual devotion. Some people practice group meditation to experience a sense of belonging. These various forms have no doubt influenced each other and led to the creation of even more methods. Some types are wrapped up in religious beliefs, while others are simply techniques that are not necessarily immersed in any belief systems, creeds, or dogmas.

There are three basic categories of meditation: focused attention or concentration, mindfulness, and effortless transcending. But within these categories exists a wide variety of practices, some of which are silent and still, and others that are vocal or involve movement.

Focused attention is all about centering the mind. It often employs some kind of a focal point, which can be anything from a mantra to a mudra to a thought or idea. Sometimes people like to employ a centering thought prior to meditation, which helps enhance concentration. When we control what we pay attention to, we can zero in on tasks we want to accomplish as well as transcendent states of being. Meditations that involve focused attention and concentration are more active and focused upon an outcome.

Mindfulness meditations are all about existing exclusively in the present moment. When you're 100 percent seated in the moment, you are able to experience heightened levels of focused attention and concentration. The difference: It's coming from a place of simply being present as opposed to a place of effort.

Meditations that involve effortless transcendence are more about putting yourself in the right place at the right time and then employing primarily non-active strategies, which will open you to spontaneous experiences of spiritual ecstasy and deep internal surrender. These transcendent experiences can be encouraged but cannot be forced.

Think of om as a key to open a door into universal consciousness.

Om is the vibrational representation of creation. It is like someone saying the words "I am." I am present. I am alive. I create. I am.

There is great power in connecting with nonreligious, non-gender-based, unbiased, pure essence energy. It is symbolic of the vibration of all existence (that we understand). It is as if everything that exists was born out of a receptive womb and om is the result.

You can tap into this essence to magnify the energy of things you would like to create in your own life. You can use the mantra om prior to a meditation designed to help you manifest results in the world.

You can also use om prior to a meditation for healing or internal growth because potential results exist in the world—they are sourced in the energy that exists in every living thing. Opportunities for healing exist in your being, mind, and heart and manifest during focused meditation. So the power of the word om can help you capitalize on the original energy that created everything.

Think about how amazing that is! One word and its vibration can open a door to the entire universe. What that really means is that you and your consciousness have the power to access anything you choose. And you can be anything you choose simply by tapping into universal energy. In fact, you possess unlimited potential and power. You are om.

The next time you settle in to begin your mantra, you will have a newfound appreciation for the history and science that make up the beauty of the om meditation. It is present in many variations of language and it appears in history in many different ways. One thing about the om meditation is certain: It is a universal sound that is representative of the unity that's needed to empathize with those around us. It's a sound and a word that encompasses all of life in a mystical and connected way.

## HINDU MEDITATION STYLES

The traditional Hindu meditative path is called raja yoga (regal yoga) and is based on the Yoga Sutras composed by Patanjali, who lived sometime during the first or second century AD (there are differing opinions as to when Patanjali lived and when exactly the Sutras were written). The school of Hinduism that developed out of these texts has had the most influence on the West. However, many Westerners hear the word *yoga* and assume it only means doing the postures or asanas—what is formally called hatha yoga. But, in fact, the system to reach enlightenment in Hindu traditions is an eight-limb approach. Just as Hinduism doesn't traditionally set the asana postures to stand alone as a practice, neither is dhyana (meditation) meant to be practiced irrespective of the other seven limbs.

In the yogic tradition, postures are an important component of meditation, because the form of meditation practiced requires being able to sit in one pose comfortably for long periods of time. The postures, part of hatha yoga, help maintain balance and harmony within the body to enable it to meditate for many hours through strength and good health.

Like some other mutually influenced meditation paths such as Jainism and Buddhism, Hinduism includes the component of restraint. This refers to curbing actions that may cause harm to other beings, both human and animal. This is where adoption of vegetarianism often comes into play. A second component, observances, deals with religious practices, such as cleanliness and attendance to scripture study.

Hindu-style yoga meditation was introduced to the West by Swami Vivekananda in the late nineteenth century. As it was passed on over the next century through various disciples of two prominent schools of thought, yoga in the United States became predominantly asana-based (posture) yoga. As Louis Komjathy put it in his book *Contemplate Literature*, yoga in the West "has much more to do with European gymnastics and Hindu nationalism in twentieth-century India than any imagined ancient Vedic Yoga."

However, despite the prevalence of asana yoga in the West, other teachers have created followings based on other limbs of the path. The Hare Krishna movement was started in the 1960s by A. C. Bhaktivedanta Swami Prabhupada, who taught that Krishna was the supreme God to be worshipped. Adherents to this following were to recite mantras and chants, and ensure that all of their actions were pleasing to Krishna.

Kriya yoga has also maintained some popularity in America. First brought to the United States by Yogananda, the kriya yoga path is a method that focuses on multiple techniques. The first step is a series of exercises that prepares the mind for meditation. Second is a concentration effort that helps the practitioner pull away from thought and focus inwardly. Then the focus is learning to concentrate on oneself and recognize the attributes of the divine self within. Lastly, the most complex technique is body control, where the practitioner slows down breathing moving into stillness.

## BUDDHIST MEDITATION STYLES

Here are several meditation styles that originated in the Buddhist tradition:

### Insight Meditation

Insight meditation, derived from the Theravada school of Buddhism, focuses on intentional watching of the mind. The intention is to keep focused awareness within the mind, and when it wanders, to gently bring it back. This type of meditation is also called mindfulness, or *vipassana*. Wonderfully nonreligious, this is a method that is very useful today.

Insight meditation has been popularized by such well-known figures as Thich Nhat Hanh. Jon Kabat-Zinn, professor emeritus of medicine at the University of Massachusetts Medical School, helped to bring mindfulness practices into the mainstream and medical world in the 1980s and beyond through his Mindfulness-Based Stress Reduction (MBSR) clinic.

## Zen Meditation

Zen meditation's roots are in the Mahayana school of Buddhism that largely grew out of Japan and Korea. This type of meditation focuses on three sub-types of practice:

1. Similar to insight meditation, the practitioner watches thoughts as they arise and disappear.
2. The student attempts to sit very quietly, doing nothing, with no thought at all.
3. The meditation student ponders a koan, or word puzzle, designed to elevate thought above dualistic thinking (a style unique to Zen).

Two major proponents of Zen in the West were Alan Watts and D. T. Suzuki. Post–World War II America proved to be fertile ground for Zen from Japan to take root in America. The 1950s saw the rise of the Beat movement in the United States, in which a group of rebel thinkers and artists were disillusioned with their culture and looked to Eastern philosophy for inspiration. The Beat revolt provided a clear entrance for Zen values into much of the American mainstream. During this period of the early 1950s, D. T. Suzuki came to the United States to lecture on Zen. His ability to translate traditional Zen texts for Americans and relate Zen to modern physics, medicine, and Christianity resonated with the intellectual population.

## Tibetan Meditation

Tibetan meditation carries many cultural trappings from Tibet and is composed of three primary components: Tibetan shamanism, traditional Buddhism, and tantric teachings from India. Tibetan meditation uses the cultural deities and tantric practices of incorporating one's own energy to help achieve a mind-body connection.

Tibetan Buddhist centers are found throughout the United States. Perhaps the most well-known contact with this type of meditation for most Americans is through the Dalai Lama. Tibetan lamas began to take on students in America in the mid-1950s. One of the most famous of these lamas was Chögyam Trungpa, who came to the U.S. in 1970 and developed an organization that would later become Shambhala International. He created over one hundred meditation centers as well as Naropa University in Boulder, Colorado. Two of his more well-known students who became teachers in their own right are Pema Chodron and Ken Wilber.

## Dzogchen Meditation

*Dzogchen* is a style of meditation that is gaining more popularity in the United States of late. Another derivative of Tibet, it attempts to discover "pure mind"—the absolute nature of reality. It is akin to many insight meditation practices in that it seeks to achieve deep awareness of the present moment, but it draws on practices like Tibetan-based visualization and tantra to help reach this goal.

Dzogchen became more popularized by the Tibetan diaspora in the early 1950s, and the fourteenth Dalai Lama is a teacher of this style. *The Tibetan Book of the Dead* is a famous early translation of the Dzogchen teaching, although it is claimed to possess many translation errors.

## MODERN-DAY CHRISTIAN MEDITATION STYLES

Although many people, even Christians, might not know it, Christianity has a rich history of meditative practices. Many of these practices developed within Christianity itself, and others were borrowed from other religious traditions. Meditation can also be synonymous with contemplative prayer in Christian practice.

Within these Christian meditation practices emerge two basic categories: cataphatic and apophatic. Cataphatic theology in Christianity refers to what God is, while apophatic describes what God is not. These two points of view then offer separate benefits when incorporated into meditation.

### Apophatic Meditation

This type of meditation in Christianity is about experiencing God without images or words or any sort of exterior help. Apophatic meditation arises from much of the writings of the early Desert Fathers and the use of mantras such as the Jesus Prayer. In this type of meditation, there is no particular goal in mind other than to take the focus off oneself and attempt to just be faithful to God.

## Cataphatic Meditation

Cataphatic prayer and meditation differ from apophatic forms because they employ images, gestures, words, postures, and/or anything that brings form to the formless. Things like using a rosary while praying, kneeling to pray, making the sign of the cross, or looking at an image to incite prayerful states are all examples of cataphatic practices.

## Forms

There are currently numerous forms of Christian meditation in the United States, and the types of practice ranges widely. The Catholic Church promotes the cataphatic practices of Eucharistic and rosary meditation, where ritual and prayers such as the Hail Mary become almost chant-like when repeated by parishioners.

## MEDITATION IN MODERN-DAY JUDAISM

The mystical branch of Judaism called Kabbalah, which developed in the eleventh century CE, contains numerous meditative and contemplative practices. These included visualizations and contemplation on the names and attributes of God. Hasidism, which developed several centuries later, also uses contemplation practices in the form of walking meditations and seclusion.

Another school of Judaism called Mussar, which was developed in the 1800s, uses meditation practices for ethical improvement.

Adherents focus on developing positive traits and virtues within themselves through the practice of watching how their minds wander—a practice that also looks a lot like mindfulness meditation.

## MEDITATION IN MODERN-DAY ISLAM

Islam has maintained mystical sides, such as Sufism, which hold meditation in high regard. Many Islamic rituals can be inherently meditative, just as those in the Jewish prayer services. Islam maintains five pillars of faith: recitation of the Muslim profession of faith, pilgrimage to the holy city of Mecca, prayer five times daily, fasting during the month of Ramadan, and the giving of charity to the poor. While each of these could just become habit or a checklist, they could also be performed in a contemplative fashion.

The mystical side of Sufism tends to shy away from more political forms of religion and focuses on inward spirituality. The path of love and relationship with the Beloved (God) are of utmost importance to Sufis, as seen in the great poetry of writers such as Rumi and Hafiz.

Sufism was brought to the United States in the 1920s by Indian-born Sufi master Hazrat Inayat Khan. His son later created the Sufi Order of the West, which was open and welcoming to teachings from all religious traditions. Other Sufi orders in the West have sprung up around specific masters, such as the Golden Sufi order with famous teacher Llewellyn Vaughan-Lee.

# OTHER POPULAR FORMS OF MEDITATION

Because of increased globalization and transmission of ideas between cultures, new meditation forms have continually popped up while older established types take on new looks with different emphases. Many of these newer forms are pure technique and can be practiced in a secular fashion. Others have their roots in specific religious traditions but no longer need to be practiced within the confines of doctrine or dogma.

## Transcendental Meditation

Although Transcendental Meditation (TM) was popularized in the 1970s in America, it has its origins in Vedic meditation and has surfaced every so often in meditation traditions. The founder of TM in the United States was Maharishi Mahesh Yogi. He was a student of the Indian teacher Swami Brahmananda Saraswati from the Shankaracharya tradition of yoga. He spent many years traveling in an effort to bring an understanding of the basic essence of meditation and so named his method Transcendental Meditation in order to free it from confusion or misunderstanding related to other methods of meditation. After almost two decades of teaching TM around the world, the first training session was held in the United States in 1970.

The basic premise behind TM is not concentration or visualization. Rather, a mantra is used lightly, and the mind is allowed to wander freely, where it will eventually reach a place of silence and rest. However, unlike many other meditation practices that can be picked up gradually without any formal instruction, TM requires specific training.

After its initial upsurge in interest, adherents dropped in the early eighties. However, TM has regained popularity in the last decade, largely due to increased accessibility for people wanting to try it, along with lowered course and instruction fees. According to some reports, over ten million people from fifty countries have learned how to meditate using TM.

## Chakra Meditation

In Hindu-based traditions such as yoga and Ayurveda, focus in spiritual practice is put on the chakras. *Chakra*, which translates from Sanskrit as "wheel" or "disk," refers to a wheel of energy. The body contains seven chakras that hold life energy called *prana*. Each of these chakras is believed to correspond to specific endocrine glands in the body. Proper alignment and energy flow through these chakras is what keeps people balanced, healthy, and full of vitality. The following are short descriptions of the seven chakras:

MULADHARA CHAKRA The root chakra is located at the base of the spine and is associated with groundedness and protection. It impacts feelings of security and stability.

SVADHIṢṬHANA CHAKRA The sacral chakra is located in the lower abdomen and is associated with creativity, sexuality, and reproduction. It opens one up to new experiences and encourages exploration of new possibilities.

MAṆIPURA CHAKRA The navel chakra is located by the solar plexus and is associated with self-confidence and strength. It stimulates happiness and power.

ANAHATA CHAKRA The heart chakra is located in the center of the chest and is associated with compassion and love. When it is open, the heart chakra allows one to express both self-love and love for others.

VISHUDDHA CHAKRA The throat chakra is located in the center of the neck and is associated with clear communication and expression. An open throat chakra promotes honesty and the ability to feel safe speaking one's mind.

AJNA CHAKRA The third eye chakra is located on the forehead above the eyebrows and is associated with spiritual awareness and psychic intuition. It helps with creative problem solving, and lowers stress levels when balanced.

SAHASRARA CHAKRA The crown chakra is located at the top of the head and is associated with enlightenment and cosmic energy. A balanced crown chakra leads to feelings of spiritual connection and well-being.

When different chakras become blocked or have decreased flow for whatever reason, the body compensates by sending more energy flow to the other chakras. This can contribute to an imbalance of energy flow, causing the body to exhibit different symptoms. Chakra meditations help one break blockages by focusing on the chakras as an integrated system and later on each individual chakra. There are different forms of chakra meditations. Some are guided and have the practitioner focus on the color associated with each chakra. Others use mudras, or special hand positions, and mantra chants.

The West was first introduced to the theory of chakra energy through translations of Indian texts in the late 1800s. However, comparisons to chakras have been made in the Eastern Orthodox teachings of hesychasm and some teachings of Kabbalah. Proponents like Deepak Chopra and the rise in popularity of Ayurveda healing and medicine have continued to bring greater awareness of chakra meditation to America.

## Walking Meditation

Walking meditation has a long history in Buddhism, and is a method of being mindful and quiet while walking, often in a prescribed pattern at a consistent pace. There are very specific forms, such as Kinhin, where practitioners walk in a counterclockwise fashion using a set breathing pattern while holding a fist covered by the other hand. Walking meditation can also be done inside, walking in circles around a room, or on a path or garden outside.

The Buddha supposedly spoke of five primary benefits of walking meditation. It teaches endurance, helps overcome drowsiness, promotes good health, aids digestion, and fosters concentration. The Thai Forest tradition of Buddhism takes these ideas very seriously, and walking meditation is a primary focus of their practice. Some Thai Forest meditation masters will do walking meditation for up to fifteen hours a day.

## Labyrinth Meditation

Labyrinth meditation is a specific form of walking meditation. Modern labyrinths are derived from Greek and Egyptian antiquity, but archaeologists have also found labyrinth art in early Indian and Native American cultures. In prehistoric times, they were believed to be traps for evil spirits, but over time they have come to be associated with pilgrimage and journeys. Early Christian churches drew labyrinths on the floors of cathedrals to be part of worship. Others have used them as a tool for contemplative prayer. In current times, they have become popular in certain groups, such as the Unitarian Universalist churches and are actively taught about by groups like the Labyrinth Society.

*Labyrinth* is often translated as "maze," but this is not what a labyrinth is intended to be, as it does not contain tricks or dead-end passages. Rather, it provides a sort of walking meditation, where someone winds through a journey to the center of the labyrinth in a symbolic leaving of the outside world, perhaps shedding troubles and sorrows. When one reaches the center of the labyrinth, a place of peace, he or she then takes the journey back to the outside world.

## Tonglen and Metta Meditations

While meditation is often viewed as a process that benefits the person practicing, there are some forms that are directed outward and are meant to benefit others. Two of these are *tonglen* meditation and *metta* meditation.

Tonglen meditation is a Tibetan Buddhist practice that has been taught by the Dalai Lama and Pema Chodron in the last several decades. The premise of tonglen is, at a very basic level, to breathe in suffering and breathe out joy. This can be done on an individual level (yourself or someone else—breathing in the perceived suffering of one person and breathing out peace and comfort toward them) or by recognizing and reacting to the suffering that occurs on a global scale. This practice, which can seem quite daunting to a beginning meditator, is not necessarily meant to individually take on suffering but rather to acknowledge and accept it. As Trungpa wrote, tonglen practice has the power to "develop the psychological attitude of exchanging oneself for others."

Metta meditation is similar to tonglen in that it is for the purpose of directing good thoughts and well wishes toward others. It can be done through the simple repetition of phrases, such as "May I be happy," and "May all beings everywhere be happy." It also includes visualizing the suffering of people that you see around you. However, metta doesn't go quite as deep as tonglen. When practicing metta meditation, one is simply sending "good vibes" more than actually attempting to receive suffering into the heart. Because tonglen is so much more intense, it is often not recommended as a practice for beginners.

## Qigong

Qigong is a traditional Chinese medicinal energy system that has existed for thousands of years. While there are many different forms of this practice, they each focus on posture/movement, breathing, and meditation. In qigong, meditation is used to open up energy flow to the body, which then helps with mind and body integration.

There are currently five broad categories of qigong practice: medical, Buddhist, Taoist, Confucian, and martial arts. Medical and Taoist traditions focus on qigong as medicine—a way to preserve the body and ensure long life. Buddhist traditions use it as a means to pursue enlightenment and liberation. Confucian qigong aims for high moral standards and increased wisdom. Finally, the martial arts qigong is specifically for perfecting ability in weapons use and self-defense, as the name implies.

The Western world was unaware of the practice of qigong until the early 1970s when Nixon improved relations with China. It took another two decades for the American public to learn more about it, when Bill Moyers did a PBS series on the topic. However, since then it has gained popularity, with millions of practitioners worldwide.

# 3

# the science of
# meditation

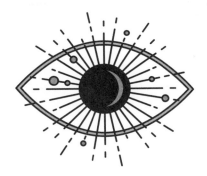

Retreats. Daily mindfulness practice. Yoga. Zen. These words have all become familiar to our Western ears. Meditation practices borrowed from Eastern traditions and philosophies have become trendy in America, and meditation is no longer just for Buddhists. In fact, many prominent companies such as Google and Apple now provide meditation training for employees. Children in some school systems are also encouraged to be mindful in their daily work and interactions with classmates. Mental-health practitioners encourage clients to spend time in regular meditation to enhance their emotional and mental well-being.

This relatively new focus has emerged out of practices developed in antiquity. Most of the major religions and philosophies that have survived over thousands of years maintain and promote their own brand of meditation practice, even though it is often called by different names. Many of these practices were passed down through numerous generations for specific groups of people using systematic training methods. Meditation was not something that the popular masses participated in regularly.

Times are changing. According to the 2012 nationwide survey "Use of Complementary Health Approaches in the U.S." by the National Institute of Health (NIH) in collaboration with the Centers for Disease Control and Prevention, 18 million American adults claim to participate in some sort of meditation. Furthermore, the number of yoga practitioners doubled over the previous decade. In fact, meditation can no longer be considered a simple hobby or spiritual self-help method practiced by people in their homes. Meditation and mindfulness have become their own big business, with industry profits brushing up against the $1 billion mark last year.

Over the course of the twentieth century and into the twenty-first, the world of science is finally catching up with what much of the religious and spiritual worlds knew all along: Very real and tangible benefits come from meditation that are not just for isolated groups of people. Furthermore, the study of meditation and its effect on humans and the world around them has become a real science in itself. With the development of brain and neurological scanning, our Western minds are finally able to glimpse what meditation can truly offer us, with the evidentiary support our culture craves.

Meditation ranges from yoga and bodywork styles to traditional "sit and pay attention to the breath" techniques. Some people meditate in an attempt to achieve enlightenment. Others do it as a method of compassion training. Still others meditate hoping to usher material wealth and success into their lives. Arguments can be made in favor of each of these outcomes, but science is now suggesting that there might be measurable physical and mental changes that arise from meditation, despite differing practices and end goals.

Determining the effectiveness and validity of meditation as a science can be challenging because of the subjectivity involved. This is most true for events that originate in the mind and are difficult to observe and test. It is even tougher for a concept like meditation that is relatively new to rigorous scientific examination, because methodologies and protocols are not yet in place. Researchers from Johns Hopkins University performed an extensive review of thousands of articles done over previous decades on the benefits of meditation and narrowed their search down to forty-seven studies that they felt were viable candidates to determine the efficacy of meditation. Like Johns Hopkins, other literature reviewers highlighted the need for improved study designs in the future. Many of the early meditation studies faced myriad problems, such as not accounting for a placebo effect, establishing inadequate control groups, and allowing other forms of biases that may have significantly influenced their data.

Despite such concerns, meditation as a topic of study within the medical world is gaining momentum. Well-known and respected meditation proponents such as Jon Kabat-Zinn and psychiatrist Bessel van der Kolk are partnering with medical institutions as Western medicine becomes more open to alternative therapies.

# 4

# meditation changes brain structure

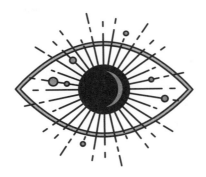

The fundamental takeaway that science has revealed about medi-tation is that it causes changes in the brain, both by way of structure and function. Studies over recent decades have repeatedly shown improvements in everything from memory to pain management. However, before highlighting these benefits, it's important to take a look at the anatomical changes that are leading to functional change.

## BRAIN TISSUE

The central nervous system in the human body, which is com-prised of the brain and spinal cord, contains two types of tissue: gray matter and white matter. Put very simply, gray matter is made up of all the nerve cells, called neurons, while white matter is made of axons, which are finger-like projections that con-nect all the neurons. Gray matter is primarily responsible for information processing in the brain; white matter helps with signal transmission.

In a 2014 review published in *Neuroscience & Biobehavioral Reviews*, a comparative analysis was done on twenty-one studies that used neuroimaging to evaluate changes in brain structure from meditation. The studies included in the review consistently showed that meditation—even relatively short stints of approximately thirty minutes a day for eight weeks—led to changes in brain-tissue volume in various gray-matter regions. These types of changes that occur in brain volume are part of a phenomenon referred to as neuroplasticity.

Neuroplasticity is the brain's ability to alter itself in order to help heal from injury or adapt to new environments. Volumed increases in certain parts of the brain can help improve various functions, while volumed decreases in specific areas can help lessen anxiety and stress responses.

Initial conclusions from a study performed earlier this year are tentatively hopeful that meditation provides positive benefits for white-matter tissue as well. White-matter changes and breakdown in older adults can play a significant role in disability outcomes and vascular disease. When white matter begins to wear out, people are at higher risk for depression, mobility problems, cardiovascular issues, and cognitive impairment. Their early findings suggest that white-matter nerve fibers may be better preserved through meditation, thus helping to maintain brain integrity throughout the aging process.

## RESOURCE ALLOCATION AND PROCESSING

The brain, as marvelous as it is, has a limited ability to focus attention on different things. However, because of neuroplasticity, the brain is able to not only modify structural points but also to adjust how it allocates its resources and sets up neural networks. One example of this is a phenomenon called an "attentional blink." An attentional blink is a gap in identification—for instance, when we are trying to process two meaningful pieces of information spaced very closely together. Our brains tend to get stuck on the first event and completely miss or gloss over the second one because of a lag in information-processing time.

"Mental Training Affects Distribution of Limited Brain Resources," a study based on participants who attended a three-month meditation retreat at the Insight Meditation Society in Barre, MA, showed that intense mental training, such as that provided by meditation, can significantly affect the attentional-blink response. Authors of the study hypothesize that mental training teaches the brain to avoid allocating all of its resources to the first event, which allows it to quickly transition focus to the second event, resulting in a shorter attentional blink. In theory, this implies that meditation could help people move their attention smoothly from one event to another without getting stuck on one and completely missing the next. A shortened attentional blink offers many real-world implications, including better self-regulation, which will be discussed next.

# MEDITATION AND EMOTIONAL HEALTH

Meditation, especially mindfulness meditation, helps promote emotional health through good self-regulation. The ability to self-regulate saves us from being tossed to and fro by external influences, circumstances, and events. When we self-regulate well, we are better able to control the trajectory of our emotional lives and resulting actions based on our values and sense of purpose. There are three important components of self-regulation that have been proposed by researchers: emotional regulation, self-awareness, and attention control.

## Emotional Regulation

Emotional regulation involves different strategies that help us navigate our emotional states. This regulation is a significant life skill, which helps us not only avoid acting on feelings rashly or dangerously but also motivate or encourage ourselves when we aren't feeling confident about our circumstances.

## Self-Awareness

Self-awareness is the ability to understand who you are as a person: your personality, motivations, strengths, and weaknesses. Self-aware people are able to live authentically, because they understand who they are in relation to themselves and others. They are also able to better understand others and how others respond to them.

## Attention Control

Attention control is just how it sounds: the ability to control where you hold your attention. This seems simple, but is in fact very difficult. Our minds get distracted very easily without training and flit here and there throughout the day. Meditation practices help our brains learn to hold a steady focus on one thing for longer periods of time.

## SELF-REGULATION

Emotional regulation, self-awareness, and attention control are nothing new to those who regularly practice meditation or to the world of psychology. But the science of how meditation actually affects brain function to promote emotional health is a relatively new field. In many cases, educated guesses are the best scientists can offer about how meditation affects emotional well-being.

When there is an emotional response in the brain, some parts are activated and other parts are suppressed. How one perceives an event leading to an emotional response also controls areas of brain activation. This phenomenon can theoretically change depending on how long someone has been meditating. For example, a meditation beginner might have the benefit of their prefrontal cortex (PFC) activating during an emotional event, whereas their amygdala calms down. The PFC is the part of the brain where we engage in complex thinking, problem solving, and planning, whereas the amygdala controls our fight-or-flight responses and is triggered when we're stressed. Research suggests that a meditation beginner's brain might learn to deal with emotion by switching over to PFC control, while someone who is experienced in meditation might no longer need the PFC to help handle big emotions. Instead, the brain of an experienced meditator is "automated" to accept emotional states without attachment. Either way, a suppressed amygdala can often help a person approach an emotional situation in a calm, more controlled fashion.

Self-awareness is a tricky area for scientists to understand, meditation aside. Self-awareness requires consciousness, for which the cerebral cortex (the gray matter covering the two hemispheres of the brain) is responsible. The cerebral cortex helps modulate many of the traits that make us human and differentiates us from other creatures with simple animal behavior. However, scenarios have been documented where people lose activity in significant portions of their cerebral cortices through injury or disease and yet behave fairly normally. Unexpected occurrences like these keep researchers puzzled as they try to map out how the brain works.

Scientists suggest that we maintain attention using several different brain networks. Attention control is achieved through three separate but interrelated networks that focus on arousal, alertness, and attentional engagement. Basically, different areas of the brain are activated when something catches your attention, other areas help you perk up and take notice, and still others help you maintain focus. One area of the brain doesn't work alone; rather, many areas work in conjunction with one another. Even when you get distracted and your mind wanders off, your brain is slipping into a default-mode network with its own activation pattern. Meditation helps retrain the brain to slip back into this default pattern less frequently, so we don't lose attention to what is going on in the present.

## EMOTIONAL HEALTH OUTCOMES

Many claims have been made about the emotional-health outcomes that result from practicing mediation. It has been associated with decreased anxiety, decreased stress response to negative stimuli, and reduced ego defensiveness. It has also been linked with better mood, decreased depression, and an overall increased feeling of well-being. Finally, meditation has been shown to help people with chronic insomnia achieve better sleep.

Meditation often has very helpful benefits for people suffering from emotional deregulation, especially for those who have experienced trauma. Transcendental Meditation (TM) in particular has been successful for people who have suffered through emotionally crippling life events. For example, the U.S. military has performed preliminary studies and found that practicing TM reduces the need for psychotropic drug prescriptions among war veterans. Survivors of the 2011 tsunami that hit Japan tested with lower stress levels after practicing TM for a ten-day period. Congolese refugees, a group of people who have experienced extreme trauma from genocide, sexual violence, and torture, have also appeared to benefit from TM, exhibiting reduced post-traumatic stress disorder (PTSD) symptoms.

Ultimately, while emotional health has been touted as a primary perk of meditation, more large, clinically-based studies need to be performed to elucidate the scientific details of how meditation is helping people feel so much better. A sizable portion of previous studies that have evaluated emotional outcomes lacked control groups, were not randomized, or were based on questionnaires and surveys, which are less subject to quality data analysis.

## MEDITATION AND PAIN MANAGEMENT

Studies have shown how meditation appears to help reduce fibromyalgia, lower-back pain, osteoarthritis, migraines, and many other types of chronic pain. However, most of these were small, preliminary studies. Researchers agree that the pathways for meditation-mediated pain relief are not well understood. Investigating pain can be a difficult undertaking, with many confounding factors and subjectivity involved, especially in how study participants tolerate and describe pain. Despite this, many are hopeful that meditation can be a real solution in light of the current opioid crisis and the need for alternative, robust pain-management solutions.

A primary question for scientists to answer is how meditation is actually helping with pain. One study performed in 2015 with a group of 109 participants found that a mindfulness/meditation pain program can offer real benefits for managing chronic pain but perhaps not tangible reduction of pain. The study evaluated the participants over a six-month period, using a meditating group and a control group.

Changes for actual pain felt by the meditation group participants were insignificant. However, the meditation participants showed an increased ability to accept the pain, feel in control of it, and maintain better mental health while experiencing pain. Much more work needs to be done in this area to better understand this scenario: Is meditation truly alleviating the pain itself, or do people learn to accept and control their pain by meditating and engaging in better self-regulation?

## MEDITATION AND BODY SYSTEM FUNCTION

Besides helping with pain management and improving mental health, meditation practices can also be beneficial for various systems in the body. It has been known for a long time that chronic stress leads to persistently high levels of cortisol in the body, which can contribute to depression, heart disease, and digestive issues, just to name a few. A constant state of highly emotional activity puts strain on the body's organs through persistent wear and tear.

A review of the effect of meditation on cardiovascular health found that meditation, even in durations as short as a week, can decrease cortisol levels in the body by reducing stress responses. The review also determined that meditation seems to positively influence lipid (fat) panels in patients as well as potentially lower the risk for heart attacks and cardiovascular diseases. Other similar reviews have found that meditation can help improve immunity by decreasing inflammation and increasing cell-mediated immune responses, which might provide some measure of protection against bacterial and viral infections.

## MEDITATION AND BEHAVIOR

Since meditation has been shown to help with emotional regulation and stress response, it seems obvious that it could help with behavioral issues. When people are emotionally well-regulated, they are less likely to act out or make rash choices. Because of this, meditation programs have been implemented in a variety of settings to help both children and adults.

Meditation training in families with autistic children is gaining more attention. The goal is to train parents to deal with their own personal issues, to train the parents and child to work together on issues in their joint relationship, and finally to help the child with his or her own triggers that lead to unwanted behaviors—all through mindfulness. Data in this area is still preliminary, but it looks hopeful that meditation may be a helpful tool to parents with children on the autism spectrum.

Another area where meditation is helping behavior is in schools. Many schools in the U.S. have implemented some sort of meditation program with several goals in mind. Meditation works within the idea of neuroplasticity, as we discussed earlier, which aids in learning. It also helps regulate emotions and can serve as a hands-off, compassionate form of discipline. Finally, it is part of an overall attitude of understanding that school and learning in general should focus on the child as a holistic person and not just as a cognitive sponge.

Meditation practices have existed for thousands of years and are unlikely to disappear. Their potential benefits are worthy of much more study in the future, and fortunately, interest in the science behind meditation has been piqued. With the high cost of prescription drugs, a lack of non-addictive, long-term pain-management options, and the increased prevalence of chronic stress in this country, meditation may be a viable part of a solution. At the very least, science has shown that meditation is capable of changing the brain in a positive manner. And when we change our brains, we can change our lives.

# 5

# meditation in india, asia, and beyond

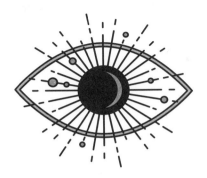

Meditation is a practice that fosters mental stamina, perseverance, and the ability to openly receive. You or someone you know may employ this technique daily to calm stress or give your mind some much-needed rest, but many people do not know how prevalent meditation was throughout many geographic regions. The earliest written records date back to 3000 BCE, when artifacts in the Indus Valley of ancient India were found showing early practitioners sitting in what today would be called meditation poses. So how did meditation survive through thousands of years of history, and why is it still being taught so many years later?

When you think of meditation, the country of India is no doubt the first place that comes to mind, and for good reason. Meditation was first recorded there in documents dating back to 1500 BCE, when meditation called Vedantism was first practiced in the Hindu religion. Vedantism comes from Vedanta, an ancient spiritual philosophy that is the foundation of the Hindu faith. It affirms the oneness of existence, divinity of the soul, and harmony of all religions.

In almost all versions of early meditation, attaining pure consciousness leads to salvation and is one of the main goals. The same can be true in Jain meditation, one of the common practices in Jainism. The ancient Indian religion of Jainism was a sixth-century movement that broke off of Hinduism and was created by Mahavira, who believed self-denial was the true path to salvation.

## MINDFULNESS IN INDIA

In 624 BC, Buddha Shakyamuni was born in Northern India, in an area that is now considered Nepal. When he was in his late twenties, he journeyed into the forest to devote his life to meditation, where he spent much time reflecting on the suffering of humanity. His teachings began to spread across India and into Asia. Today, Buddhism is one of the four largest religions in the world. Meditation is a core component of the religion, which uses mindful concentration to reach enlightenment and ultimate nirvana. Buddhism focuses on four important elements: salvation of morality, contemplative concentration, knowledge, and liberation. There are different forms of Buddhist meditation, including Tibetan, Zen, and Theravadan. Buddhist meditation is responsible for much of the way we view meditation today, like our mental picture of the correct way to sit during meditation.

In the fifteenth century, a monotheistic religion called Sikhism was created in India. Its main principle is that one God rules the universe and all of humanity is considered equal. A big component of the religion is the thought that eternal salvation is reached only through meditation.

## SPREADING PEACE TO ASIA

Taoism was prevalent in Asia around the same time Buddhism was holding strong in India. Taoism is also known as Daoism and is a religion based on the *Dao De Jing*, a political and philosophical text. Followers of Taoism strive to live in harmony, known as Tao or Dao. The meditation techniques, much like those of Buddhism, focus on four main areas, including concentration, mindfulness, contemplation, and visualization. The Daoism faith also uses meditation in their martial arts. Thanks to the Silk Road, Taoism and Buddhism spread across Asia.

## STILLNESS IN THE MIDDLE EAST

The second largest religion in Iran besides Islam is called Bahá'í Faith. The religion was founded in the early nineteenth century by Mirza Husayn-'Ali Nuri, known as Bahá'u'lláh, which means "glory to God" in Arabic. It branched off of Shi'ite Islam and was founded in Persia. The religion focuses on prayer and reflection and requires a strong service to humanity. The religion also greatly favors girls receiving education. According to the article titled "What Bahá'ís Believe: The Life of the Spirit," meditation requires focused reflection that helps give the follower a defining sense of self and brings new insight into practical matters. Sadly, Bahá'í Faith followers located in Iran are currently facing terrible persecution for their beliefs.

The largest religion in the Middle East is Islam. It is a monotheistic, faith-based religion built on the revelations of Muhammad as the Prophet of Allah found in the Quran. Meditation is widely and devotedly practiced throughout the Islamic faith. Meditation revolves around finding the oneness of God. Islam focuses on five areas of meditation: contemplation, reflection, concentration, observation, and presence of mind.

## MINDFULNESS IN JUDAISM AND CHRISTIANITY

By the Middle Ages, meditation was starting to sprout up in the Jewish religion, though it existed with the creation of the Torah in Babylonian times. In the eleventh century, with the rise of Kabballah, Jewish meditation began to spread rapidly throughout the Jewish community. When taken as a whole, Jewish meditation encompasses several different versions of traditional practices, including personal prayer, contemplation, prayer-seeking communion, esoteric combinations of divine names, and emotional insight. It also calls for an understanding of philosophical concepts and ethical reasoning.

Jewish mystics practice the idea of centering away from the self and toward the divine hand in all things. Jewish meditation can be more rigorous than the mainstream relaxation forms and can involve focusing on letters of the Hebrew alphabet.

Meditation began to pop up in Eastern Christianity in the early Byzantine Period and then again in the tenth and eleventh centuries as the idea of hesychasm (the repetition of the Jesus Prayer) took hold and spread throughout the religion. Eastern Christianity saw meditation as a form of constant prayer and reflection. Meditation in Western Christianity began in the sixth century, when Benedictine monks began a form of Bible reading called Lectio Divina, which is Latin for "divine reading." In the twentieth century, meditation became more prominent, and the practice of Lectio Divina became more mainstream. Reflective prayer and meditation is still used in Christianity today.

## THE METAMORPHOSIS OF SECULAR AND NEW AGE MEDITATION

In the twenty-first century, meditation is practiced by those with religious affiliations as well as the general public. Meditation is taught as a stress-reducing technique that helps provide self-reflection, patience, and centering. In his book *Secular Meditation: 32 Practices for Cultivating Inner Peace, Compassion, and Joy*, Rick Heller explains that secular meditation is all about finding a way to show empathy and appreciate life by living in the right here and right now.

The New Age movement is the philosophy that the divine lives in each one of us, manifesting in different ways. New Age meditation combines the ideas from traditional forms of meditation and yoga and blends it with new practices such as stress reduction, positions, and exercise. Though an age-old technique, only eight percent of the population claimed to practice yoga in a 2007 NIH study. The same study found that a surprising 1.6 percent of children used meditation in 2012. That's an increase of 202,000 children since 2007.

Though initially started to bring religious groups closer to the divine and the right path to salvation, meditation has since branched off into many different forms and techniques. As history has moved through Buddhism to Judaism to Christianity, meditation has remained a constant in all the different religions and philosophies. One other thing that hasn't changed is the positive effect it has on the body and mind as a whole. According to the National Center for Complementary and Integrative Health, "Meditation is a mind and body practice that has a long history of use for increasing calmness and physical relaxation, improving psychological balance, coping with illness, and enhancing overall health and well-being." Practicing daily mindfulness and meditation can help reduce anxiety, depression, and insomnia; lower blood pressure; and fight off lingering pain in cases of fibromyalgia. The mind-body connection and the benefits of meditation can't be ignored. "The benefits of the practice extend beyond the personal to enrich relationships with others, with one's community, and with the world," says Heller. That's a perfect step for an ancient practice that's been known to put the love of others above self.

# 6

# *om:* the universal sound

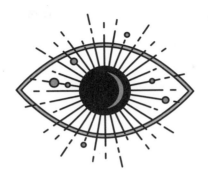

If you look at the creation of the Earth, you'll see that all the forces of physics combined to create an ebb and flow that keeps everything running in a continuous, harmonious circle of life. Like a well-oiled machine, we've all been connected since the beginning of time through a beautiful, mystical process of unity. And, since the beginning, we've all been dancing to the beat of one certain drum—a vibration, really. If we were to put that very vibration into words, it would simply be *om*, a universal sound respected by all religions and uttered by many reflective souls.

*Om*, written in Hindu as *aum*, is the most sacred sound and most recognized symbol in Hinduism. It represents the infinite energy of divinity and depicts how we can all live in a world of harmony. Known by some as the "primordial vibration" of the entire universe, including ourselves, it provides a space for all of philosophy and mythology to meet and dwell together. In fact, it precedes and ends almost every Hindu incantation or mantra. The universal sound of *om* has been found in manuscripts and writings since the creation of the Vedic traditions of Hinduism, Jainism, and Buddhism. According to the *International Journal of Yoga*, the descriptions of *om* have been taken from four Upanishads (*Mundaka*, *Mandukya*, *Svetasvatara*, and *Katha*), the *Bhagavad Gita*, and Patanjali's *Yoga Sutras*. In Christianity, *om* is the start of omega, the beginning and the end, and can also be found in the word *amen*. The Indian scriptures regard the sacred syllable *om* as the primordial sound from which all other sounds emerge, which signifies *om* as the Supreme Power.

*Om* is the expression of all the sounds in the universe and blends to form a perfect, continuous humming. How does this work? Earth's physics help keep everything moving in a continuous circle—up and down, right and left, rinse and repeat—and the sound of *om* is structured the same way. The *om* meditation consists of three letters (*A*, *U*, and *M*) that cover the entire scope of the way we've learned to articulate through spoken language. *Om* as *aum* is actually structured by four sounds. The *A* sound comes from your throat but starts in your stomach. The *U* originates in the chest and requires the help of the tongue. The *M* sound stems from your head and comes out through a vibration in your lips. The last sound is merely silence, when the lungs have run out of air but the word still lingers on the body. *Om* is natural for you to say because it consists of every sound you've ever learned to make as a child. The beginning—when the sound originates in the stomach area—is representative of the creation of all mankind. The *U* represents the ability for your body to breathe in new life and preserve the life you currently lead. The *M* shows that all change must first happen in the mind. The silence is representative of the stillness that brings about reformation and salvation.

With roots in mythology and also ties to the Trimurti (the trinity) in Hinduism, the *aum* sound is also representative: The *A* is Brahma's golden nucleus; the *U* is Vishnu, who was holding Brahma on a lotus, just like how your torso sustains your head; and the *M* is the final cycle of existence.

There are plenty of benefits to be had by correctly practicing the mantra of *om*. Studies concerning autonomic and respiratory processes show that while the mind concentrates on the *om* meditation, the body is combining mental alertness with physiological rest. This can help neurons in the brain have a clear path for processing. Meditation has also been proven to slow the heart rate and calm breathing. Chanting *om* reduces stress and boosts relaxation. A study performed at the Lady Irwin College in New Delhi says chanting *om* can help athletes predict dehydration, meaning awareness of their bodily functions improves thanks to the sensitivity that comes from *om*.

One thing about the *om* meditation is certain: It is a universal sound that is representative of the unity that's needed to empathize with those around us. It's a sound and word that encompasses all of life in a mystical and connected way.

# 7

# the inner witness

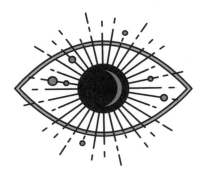

The inner monologue voice. We all have it. It's that nagging voice that's always chattering away inside your head. It's the same voice that is saying the words you are reading right now so that it feels like you are hearing them in your head. How many times per day does that voice ask or say something to distract you from what is actually happening in your life in the present moment?

*I should go to the gym. I'm getting so lazy.*

*Why hasn't he called me back? He must not like me anymore.*

*I don't know why I bother doing this work; it doesn't mean anything.*

That inner voice can talk us through difficult situations. It can help us make the list that we need to have a successful day. It can help us navigate subtle emotional nuances with our friends and family. It is our personality self. It's the part of us that's in the forefront, thinking and doing.

In *The Untethered Soul* by Michael Singer, this phenomenon of mind chatter taking control of your life is known as your "inner roommate." The inner roommate lives in your head, dictating your thoughts, your reactions, and your emotional state. How do we turn down the volume on this inner chatter? How do we rise out of the negative thinking that our mind chatter can feed? Who is responsible for this mind chatter, anyway? Is it you? Is the inner voice who you are?

The external world plays a massive part on the influence of the chatter in our mind. Between what we are fed through social interactions and consumption of all kinds of media, our inner monologue is constantly being fed and thrives off persistent stimulation. So much of what we see and hear from the media is telling us that who we are simply isn't good enough. This couldn't be further from the truth! We are all beautiful expressions of creative and benevolent universal energy.

This isn't to say that we don't have any issues. We all have problems, some of which are more serious. But some of these problems are simple parts of human existence that get inflated through the cycle of listening to our chaotic inner thoughts.

## BECOMING YOUR INNER WITNESS

The problem with the inner roommate is how we think that, because it's in our head, living within us, it's a part of us. But what if we could picture that inner roommate as an actual entity outside of our bodies? Thinking of the inner roommate as separate is the first step in shifting our awareness into a deeper conscious state. As we move to the state of witnessing the object of disturbance rather than *being* the object of disturbance itself, we create an objective awareness. This creation starts to separate ourselves from this mental disturbance. This isn't to say that the problems you experience will disappear. They will continue to exist. But as you create this division and develop objectivity toward what you are witnessing, you can control its level of influence on your thoughts and start to move toward a place of inner peace. When you rewire your consciousness to see things for what they really are, rather than seeing them with a false lens influenced by outside factors, you are allowing yourself to bear witness. As you bear witness, you can move to a different frame of reference with ease and discernment rather than get involved with what the thoughts are saying. You can move into a place of responsibility and ownership rather than getting lost in the vortex of the problem itself.

As you sit in meditation, allow yourself to relax more deeply and let the mind chatter fall away. Then, if you just sit back in yourself a little bit, you can begin to feel what's behind the personality self. Relax your heart and feel that behind all of the mind chatter is your silent, inner-witness presence. It is pure peace, and it is your divine soul—your highest self. It is eternally present. It is the part of you that existed before entering the body you currently inhabit, and it will exist after you exit that body. This is your inner witness.

# 8

# meditations to open your heart and mind

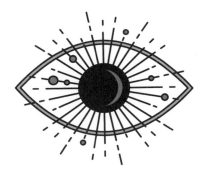

In this next section, you will learn tools and tricks of the trade to learn how to meditate. You will discover how to set the scene and position yourself for optimum relaxation and awakening. Meditation is the process of entering into a receptive state and letting the goodness of the universe fill you. It is dipping your toe into a pool of infinite stillness.

In deep meditation, people sometimes experience the powerful phenomenon of surrender. When we surrender in a spiritual sense, we let go of all effort and strain and instead are open to receive. Sometimes when we settle into the experience of surrender, we feel spontaneous bursts of forgiveness toward others, ourselves, and existence. Meditation can open the door and welcome all of the unfathomably vast goodness in the universe.

# CREATING A MEDITATION SPACE

You can meditate anywhere and anytime! You do not need any fancy supplies or equipment. All you need are a few minutes and a desire to quiet your mind. In the middle of a hectic day—after parking your car, for instance—you can take sixty seconds to sit in silence and focus your mind before beginning the next activity. As you lay down to go to sleep, you can spend a few minutes meditating in the comfort of your own bed.

Some people like to create a dedicated area in which to meditate, especially if beginning a serious practice. Some people have a little meditation area in a corner of their bedroom or even a meditation room in their home. Things you might have in this area include the following:

A MEDITATION CUSHION is designed to raise your pelvis up a few inches so that you can sit comfortably in a cross-legged position.

THROW PILLOWS can be nice if you are leaning against the wall, or they can be substituted for a meditation cushion.

BLANKETS are always nice to have on hand in case you get cold while sitting in stillness for an extended period of time.

CHIMES OR BELLS can have a clearing effect on the space in which you will be meditating. You can use the gentle sounds created by these instruments to set the stage for your meditation.

A YOGA MAT is useful if you would like to meditate while lying down or are going to combine your meditation with yoga.

ESSENTIAL OILS are a lovely way to indulge in a little self-care and prepare your body for meditation.

CRYSTAL OR BRONZE SINGING BOWLS are used to harmonically clear energy from spaces. They are also used to harmonize the energy of the body, which is a great thing to do before, during, or after meditating.

A JOURNAL is great to have nearby in case any insights occur to you during your meditation and also to record any experiences you may have during your time meditating.

## MEDITATION BODY POSITIONS

You can meditate in any position. The most commonly used position is one where you sit cross-legged. This is a derivative of the lotus pose in yoga. The idea of sitting cross-legged or in the lotus position is that you are keeping your energy in a closed circuit by having your legs touch each other. That means none of your energy or vital life force can leak away. In this position, people often place their hands in their laps in various positions. One common hand placement is to have both hands faceup, lay one on top of the other, and then join the two thumbs gently above that, forming a circle. This, too, is intended to create a closed circuit for the energy of your body. This helps keep your energy internal instead of having it go out of your body and interact with the world around you, because meditation is a process of going within.

You can also meditate during your yoga practice in various body positions. People also do moving meditations, which place the body in all kinds of interesting positions. We will learn about those later in the book.

It is also equally effective to meditate lying down. You can do this on a yoga mat with a cushion under your knees and a pillow under your head. You can even meditate in bed.

## SEALING UP AFTER YOU MEDITATE

Some people like to seal up their energy fields after they complete a meditation. This helps you keep the good energy in and not be too open as you go back out into the world. You do not have to do this every time you meditate. It is mostly recommended if you feel spacey or less present afterward, or if you have been doing one of the guided meditations provided in Chapter 9, page 85.

I also like to use this process before entering crowded places, like airports and malls. This is especially helpful for people who are highly sensitive to other people's energy.

An essential presleep ritual is to seal up your being. Sometimes we are very open, and while we sleep, we need to rest. That openness can be distracting and get distorted while we are trying to process our subconscious emotions through dreams. Here is a way to quiet some outside energy and seal your space:

Say this aloud or internally: "*I seal and protect all wormholes, portals, doorways, and openings in my physical and energetic bodies in all dimensions, interdimensions, and all realities as needed for my highest good and the highest good of all life for all time. I own my space and only that which is of the light may enter. It is done.*"

## HOW TO MEDITATE BY WATCHING YOUR THOUGHTS

Sit in a comfortable meditation position and close your eyes. Closing your eyes helps to tune out the visual stimulation of the outside world. You are endeavoring to sit and be present and allow your mind to relax. Inevitably, thoughts will arise. It's natural for that to happen. When a thought arises, you can imagine placing it on a log and setting it to flow down a swift yet tranquil stream. Alternatively, when a thought arises, you can let it float away on a fluffy cloud. Just like when you look at the sky, clouds will pass by; it's natural. So it is with your thoughts. As thoughts arise, your job is not to get attached to the thought or engage with it—just watch it, notice it, and then let it float downstream or be swept away by a gentle wind.

Simply sit in quiet. Allow your mind to be clear and present. Each time a thought arises, let it float away. Watch it arise, and watch it be released. This is watching your thoughts. It's a wonderful exercise to become connected with the present moment. As you rest in the present moment, you may spontaneously feel your consciousness sit back a little bit and then you will get to experience your own inner witness.

## HOW TO MEDITATE BY FOLLOWING YOUR BREATH

Sit in a comfortable position. You can have your back against the cushion of a couch or chair or lie down as needed. When you first try this meditation, sometimes it's easier to do it sitting up.

Take a deep and long inhalation through your nose. Feel the air first go all the way down into your abdomen and fill that area up so that your abdomen moves outward. In that same inhalation, feel the middle part of your lungs (the thoracic area) fill and then your upper chest and the top of your lungs, so the inhalation starts from the bottom and fills your torso like a bag of air.

When you exhale, feel like you are squeezing the bag out from the top to the bottom. Your exhalation should be longer than your inhalation. Try to exhale the air in a slow, steady stream. You can exhale through your nose if that is comfortable or through your mouth if you need.

This is a very simple form of complete abdominal breathing. Start repeating that breathing cycle. Do that for a few minutes. Now bring awareness to your nostrils, to the area where the air comes in, and notice the sensation of the air flowing in. Feel the air enter, and bring your awareness down and through your lungs, like you're traveling with the air. As you exhale, feel your awareness travel up through your lungs and back out of your nostrils. Entrain your awareness with the air moving in and out of the body. This is following your breath.

Practice this type of meditation to clear your mind and help you focus. This also properly oxygenates your body. Oxygen is good for your health!

## MANTRA MEDITATIONS

A mantra is a word or sound that is repeated to bring focus to the mind and aid in concentration during meditation. When meditating at a moment when the mind might typically wander, a mantra can be repeated. This gives the mind something relatively singular to focus on so it doesn't get distracted.

Sanskrit is the original language of India. Many of the common mantras that you may hear about through yoga or popular-culture mentions of meditation are in Sanskrit. But a mantra can be in any language. It can also simply be a sound.

The root of *mantra* in Sanskrit is *manas*, or "the linear-thinking mind," and *tra*, or "to cross over." Mantras are believed to replace negative energy with positive energy. Sound is the first element that makes up the human body according to Indian metaphysical tradition. The purpose of repeating the mantra is to help your brain transcend your busy mind. Awareness can build by repeating the mantra.

## HOW TO MEDITATE USING A MANTRA

Begin by getting comfortable in whatever meditation position works for you. Next, take a few minutes to quiet your mind and follow your breath. Then begin gently repeating the mantra of your choice. Just allow it to rise from your divine mind.

If your mind is wandering often, repeat the mantra more frequently. Use it as a tool to focus and relax your mind at the same time. You can do this for as long as you'd like. You might start by meditating with a mantra for ten minutes and eventually work up to thirty minutes or more. When your meditation feels complete, simply stop repeating the mantra, sit for a few minutes to allow your energy to reintegrate, and then go about your day.

The mantra you choose can have a powerful effect on your being. You can consciously choose a mantra that will align with your intention. Enjoy meditation's numerous health benefits and choose a simple mantra like the words *love*, *om*, or *sat nam*. As you'll see in the list below, there are many mantras that can be used for many purposes.

Some examples of mantras include:

SAT NAM truth

OM the very first sound that the universe ever made

SHANTI MANTRA peace

ONG NAMO GURU DEV NAMO *I bow to the creative energy of the infinite. I bow to the divine channel of wisdom.*

RA MA DA SA SA SAY SO HUNG A mantra used to send healing energy to oneself and others. The literal translation is: *Sun, Moon, Earth, Infinity, All that is infinity, I am thee.*

OM NAMAH SHIVAYA *I bow to Shiva, the supreme deity of transformation who represents the truest, highest self.*

SABBE SATTA SUKHI HONTU *May all beings be well (happy).*

KARUNA HUM *I am compassion.*

ANANDA HUM *I am bliss.*

EEM HREEM SHREEM *I am the richness that I desire.*

Affirmations can also be used as mantras. Some examples of affirmations are:

*I am my higher self.*
*I am light.*
*I am peace.*
*I am radiant health.*
*I am joyfully in the divine flow of goodness.*

## LOVING KINDNESS MEDITATION

Softness. Giving. Devotion to Mother Earth and all of her beings. The sweetness that you feel when a stranger smiles at you and you automatically smile back. Or that heartbeat you feel when you witness a truly selfless act, either from you, toward you, or around you. Maybe it's just the simple feeling of relief and compassion that comes with the exchange of a hug. All of these elements are acts of Loving Kindness.

Loving Kindness, or metta, is a practice that is inherently kind, selfless, gracious, and full of heart and tenderness. It is a practice that can be directly transferred to meditation. A meditation that is grounded in Loving Kindness, or metta, mentally sends intentions of goodwill, love, and benevolence from the practitioner to a receiver.

However, a metta meditation is not linear, meaning it is not one direct line of sending and receiving. The important key to metta is that the practitioner must cultivate kindness, love, and goodness toward his or her own self before sending the same out to others.

Metta without personal love for oneself does not exist. Metta can only be founded in its most sympathetic and authentic form when it comes from the most humble and truest of intentions. The process of reaching the state where a practitioner can send metta generally starts with repeating a series of mantras that focus on establishing a circulating flow of love and kind feelings. Once these feelings are established, they can be mentally and energetically sent out, and the receipt is pure and calm.

## Early Beginnings

The word *metta* is Pali for *loving kindness*. Pali is the language of Theravada Buddhism, which is practiced across Southeast Asia in countries like Thailand, Myanmar, Cambodia, Laos, Sri Lanka, Vietnam, Nepal, Bangladesh, and parts of China.

But the early beginnings of the concept of metta did not start with Buddhism. Originally, Loving Kindness went by the Sanskrit term *maitri* and first started to appear in philosophical and written texts known as the Upanishads. These texts and philosophical ideas mark the end of the Vedic era of Hinduism, somewhere between 800 BCE and 500 BCE, as Hinduism entered into Vedanta and also gave birth to the non-duality spiritual practices. It was about this same time—somewhere around 563 BCE—that a man named Siddhartha Guatama was born in Nepal.

Siddhartha Guatama came from Aristocratic means and lifestyle. His family was luxurious and royal, and Siddhartha was afforded many of the finer things in life. His father, a king, shielded Siddhartha from seeing any type of sickness and death.

The king took extreme measures to ensure that Siddhartha would never experience suffering. But, like anything in hiding, the truth was to be discovered. The story goes that in his early twenties, Siddhartha encountered a decrepit old man on one of his horse-riding adventures. He encountered a diseased person on a second ride. Then there was a corpse. And, finally, he encountered a monk with a shaven head, a robe, and a bowl who showed him a life of withdrawal from the world. In that, Siddhartha saw freedom. He saw that aging, disease, suffering, and death were unavoidable. But he begged the question, "Life is subject to age and death. Where is the realm of life in which there is neither age nor death?"

And with that, Siddhartha left behind his riches in search of enlightenment through life in the forest for six years. It was in the forest where Siddhartha took deeply to meditation and experienced a state of enlightenment. After sharing his learnings and understandings from his time in the forest, people would ask if he was a god, an angel, or a saint. He would say no. They would ask, "Then what are you?" He would say . . .

"I am awake."

And that is how Siddhartha Guatama became Buddha. The Sanskrit root *budh* means "to wake up" and "to know." In other words, it was a turning point toward non-duality, which started to pave the way toward Buddhism from the foundation of Hinduism.

But what exactly is non-duality? Non-duality, or non-dualism, is the belief system that everything is one. It literally translates to "not two." In terms of Buddhist and Vedantic as non-dualism belief systems, "God/universe" and "self" are not separate. They are the same and live in the same place—a person is one with every thing, every one, and with the universal self. In short, Buddha's principle teachings are that all of life is *dukkha*, or suffering. But in suffering, you have everything you need, everything you search for, and zeverything to end suffering within you. There is no past, there is no future; there is only right now, in the present.

Buddha's practical approach to ending suffering—by cultivating what is already within—leads to the development of metta. Buddha's teachings have stood the test of time, and because of its practicality, Buddhism has evolved into a major belief system spanning much of the planet. And because Buddhism is non-exclusionary, people from any and all religions and spiritual belief systems (including atheists) can practice and incorporate Buddhist concepts and ideas. The idea is not to bow down to a god or deity through ritual. The teaching is to tap into what's within you—the universe that resides inside of you—and to share that with all fellow beings on this Earth, as well sharing with Earth herself.

Everywhere you turn is an element of sharing and sending love. The idea of metta has intertwined into popular culture as well. With celebrities like Russell Brand sharing his positive outcomes from meditation, Russell Simmons building a yoga center, Jennifer Aniston boasting the positive effects of her meditation practice, and Pharrell Williams getting the whole world to sing "Clap along if you feel like happiness is the truth," there is no denying that metta has seeped into the fibers of our beings. T-shirts are emblazoned with sayings like "Spread Love," "Free Hugs," "Love Leads the Way," and so on. The talk in social media and in communities is abundant with ways of how to lead with love and to rise above through keeping others in our hearts. Even in these very confusing times, love still seems to come out on top, is still the desire of humans worldwide, and is still the wish from people everywhere out to everyone—to be happy and free.

## How to Practice Metta / Loving Kindness Meditation

Get comfortable in the meditation position of your choosing. Spend a few minutes following your breath. As you become aware of your breathing, start to deepen the breath; a long inhale, followed by an even longer exhale. As the breath deepens, bring your awareness to your heart center. Start to acknowledge any discomfort that may arise, such as mental blockages or self-judgment. Simply acknowledge and seek a place of rising above. Know that you are the epitome of greatness and love.

As the judgment dissipates, repeat to yourself the following:
*"May I be free from suffering.*
*May I be happy.*

*May I be safe and protected.*

*May I live with joy and ease."*

Repeat this for about two to three minutes. Allow the mantra to integrate into the fibers of your being.

As you keep this mantra for yourself, think of someone in your life who is selfless and embodies kindness and unconditional love. This can be a parent, a grandparent, a teacher, a mentor—someone who you respect effortlessly.

Repeat the same mantra, but for this person:

*"May _____ be free from suffering.*

*May _____ be happy.*

*May _____ be safe and protected.*

*May _____ live with joy and ease."*

Repeat this for about two to three minutes. Again, allow it to integrate into the fibers of your being.

Next, move on to a neutral person for another two to three minutes. This person can be anyone you've encountered but for whom you have no specific or particular feelings. They can be someone from the grocery store, the coffee shop, or even just a passerby on the street.

The next person you send metta to should be a person of difficulty in your life, someone about whom you maybe have negative feelings. Again, repeat the mantra for another two to three minutes. This time, add in a little modification to the mantra:

*"To the best of my ability, I wish _____ to be free from suffering.*

*To the best of my ability, I wish _____ to be happy.*

*To the best of my ability, I wish _____ to be safe and protected.*

*To the best of my ability, I wish _____ to live with joy and ease."*

And finally, for the last two to three minutes, collect all of the metta to send to all beings. Repeat the mantra:

*"Lokha samastah sukhino bhavantu. May all beings everywhere be happy and free."*

You can make this practice more nuanced by selecting subcategories of people or animals as you'd like. As long as it's loving and kind, it will be freedom, it will be heart, it will be soft and devotional, and, most of all, it will be felt.

## MOVING MEDITATIONS

A moving meditation helps bring focus to your mind while integrating the energy of "divine mind" into your physical body through movement. Divine mind is the infinite, all-encompassing, high vibrational mind of the universe. It is the essence of boundless intelligence in the form of pure-white light.

When we meditate while moving, we are able to connect with varied and deep parts of ourselves. We are able to integrate new energies into our bodies through movements and focus.

### Dancing

To embark upon a dancing meditation, choose some uplifting music. Depending upon the nature of the meditation you desire, you could choose instrumental music that is peaceful, New Age music, chanting, or other types of music that bring you joy. That might include popular songs that are all about happiness, joy, and/or self-love.

Once you start your music, allow yourself to begin moving. You might want to choose a mantra to repeat if your mind wanders while you're dancing. You could choose one related to the music that you're listening to, especially if the music has words and you'll likely find yourself singing along.

The purpose of this type of meditation is to focus upon a singular intention, like "experiencing the energy of love in the core of your being," and then integrate it into your body. So if you are dancing to instrumental music, you might repeat the word *love* like a mantra as you dance.

This is a freestyle dance, so it's really about letting your body move and express itself with as little conscious thought as possible. It's not about how you look or how the dance looks, it's about the shapes and movement of the body to integrate the energy that you are intending to experience.

When you are ready to complete this meditation, turn your music off and sit in silence for a few minutes. Notice the sensations in your body. Notice if any thoughts or feelings arise. Let yourself go into a few minutes of restful meditation, and follow your breath or repeat the mantra you were using during your dance. Let the energy of the meditation settle and integrate into your body before you go about your day.

## Mudras

The word *mudra* translates as "gesture." Common uses of mudras include incorporation into yoga exercises, which have their own health benefits, and opening of chakra centers or improving the way they work. They can be used in this way as part of meditation or they can be the complete focus of meditation. Mudras have long been incorporated into traditional Indian dances, which can be used as meditation in motion.

Mudras are based on the concept that each finger stands for an element in Eastern philosophy. The thumb is fire, the index or pointer finger is wind, the middle finger is space, the ring finger is earth, and the little finger is water. More than that, each of these nerve-rich digits connects to a different part of your brain, which, in turn, corresponds to various parts of your body.

All mudras work using certain basic principles. For example, when the thumb is touched lightly to another finger, then that element is balanced. To enhance the element, point the thumb toward the base of the finger. To reduce or suppress the element, the thumb should press on the nail of that finger. For example, water is the element often associated with emotion, motherhood, and the ocean, which is a great source of life. To balance this feminine principle, lightly touch the thumb to the little finger. Sit in a relaxed meditation pose and hold this hand gesture, with the backs of your hands resting lightly on your thighs. To enhance it, to feel more, place the thumb at the base of the little finger. To suppress it, place the thumb over the nail of the little finger and hold it down. One reviewer of mudras compared them to using the hands to program the brain the way one would use a remote to program a television.

## HOW TO MEDITATE USING MUDRAS

Begin by getting in a comfortable meditation position of your choosing, and spend a few minutes following your breath. Then place your hands in any of the mudras listed below for as long as you would like. Notice the way the energy of your body feels as you place your hands in these positions. Do you notice pulsating or tingling sensations? Do you feel an increase in well-being or mental stamina? Just observe yourself, and record any observations in your journal if you choose.

Here is a list of some useful mudras you might like to try during your meditation practice:

GYAN represents the union of the elements space and air. This is the mudra that you most often see people employing when meditating. Its purpose is to enhance concentration and sharpen memory. To place your hands in this mudra, touch the tip of your thumb to the tip of your index finger, leaving your other three fingers relaxed and mostly straight.

SHUNI represents the union of space and fire. This mudra uses the purifying power of fire to balance your emotions and thoughts. When your mind is clear, your intuition is enhanced, and this mudra is used specifically to enhance intuition and awareness. It can also heighten your senses. To employ this mudra, place the tip of your thumb in contact with the tip of your middle finger, and let the other three fingers rest in a mostly straight position.

SURYA represents the union of space and water, but it is actually used to increase the solar fire element in the body. It is a warming mudra. It activates digestive and metabolic fire energy and warms those systems, thereby enlivening them. This mudra may raise the core temperature of your body, and some people use it to prevent the common cold. To place your hands in the position for this mudra, bend your ring fingers in toward your palms and place the tips of your thumbs on top of your ring fingers' outer knuckles. Let the others three fingers rest in a relatively straight position.

PRANA represents the union of the space and water elements. This mudra awakens divine energy within you. It brings forth any dormant spiritual energy so that you can feel it in a more magnified and cohesive manner. It unites spirit and divinity with human emotion and symbolizes the idea of existing as a spiritual being in a body. To position your hands in this mudra, join the tips of your thumbs with the tips of your ring and little fingers, leaving your remaining two fingers relaxed and relatively straight.

HAKINI represents the gentle union of all five elements. It is used to bring about spiritual and emotional well-being. You place your hands in this position by touching the fingertips of each finger on your right hand to the same finger on your left hand. This is a balancing and harmonizing mudra.

KUBERA represents uniting all the elements and strengthening matter and/or thought. Kubera is a Hindu deity of wealth. This mudra is especially useful to help you manifest something specific. People bring their hands into this mudra sometimes during daily life, when they are trying to find or obtain something, like a parking spot or the right size and color curtains. To use it for manifestation, picture your wish or goal in your mind and also create a very clear verbal description of it. Ask that your wish be only for the highest good. As you put your wish or goal into words, phrase it in an affirmative manner, like, "*I easily find the perfect new job and love working there. I make at least [dollar amount] and have a harmonious and joyful relationship with all my coworkers.*" And then bring your hands into the Kubera mudra. This mudra also opens the frontal sinuses and helps decongest them. Place your hands in this mudra by bringing together the tips of your thumb, index finger, and middle fingers. Then bend your ring and little fingers in toward the palms so they make gentle contact with the middle of your hand.

## Walking Meditation

Walking meditations have been popular for many hundreds of years. The physical act of walking provides us with a lovely rhythmic movement upon which we can focus. We mindfully concentrate on each step that we take during a walking meditation. We spend time being present in our environment during a walking meditation.

This type of meditation gives us the opportunity to practice mindfulness, and walking is a wonderful way to build that skill. Not only can we get a little bit of light exercise and some fresh air, but we can also practice the joyful, healing skill of being mindful.

### HOW TO PRACTICE WALKING MEDITATION

Dress comfortably and select an outdoor path that you feel safe traversing. If that's not possible, you can also practice a walking meditation in your home or any indoor space.

As you begin walking, bring your attention to the soles of your feet. Feel as if you inhabit the space between the ground and the bottoms of your feet and get into the rhythm of your steps. Allow that sensation to permeate your senses, and let your mind become quieter.

You may choose to walk very slowly, or you may choose to walk quickly. Either speed provides a wonderful opportunity for mindfulness. Next, bring your attention upward, and notice the world around you. If you are in your home, notice where you are and what you see, and if you're outside, take a look around, listen to the sounds, notice any aromas, and notice how the air feels on your body and skin.

The purpose of a walking meditation is to be mindful of what is happening as you walk and be present only to that. Just like in any other meditation, if your mind starts to wander, just gently bring it back. Practice being present as you walk. A walking meditation is a symbol of being present as you move forward through life. It's a symbol of bringing mindfulness into linear time, which is bringing spirit into body. It is traversing duality with grace and mindfulness.

# 9

# guided visualization meditations

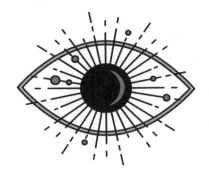

Guided visualizations are structured meditations created with a specific purpose in mind. To practice the guided visualizations contained in this book, you can begin by entering a meditative state and following your breath. Then you can follow the instructions contained in each section for the guided meditation of your choosing.

## GUIDED MEDITATION FOR FORGIVENESS

The act of forgiving can seem massive to us at times. But forgiving really is an act of simply letting go. It is releasing our attachment to the anger, sadness, or resentment that we may feel about something or someone (including the self). Think of forgiving as a simple act of relaxation. From relaxation, release will occur. And from releasing, the spiritual experience of surrender can spontaneously spring forth. Forgiveness is less about trying to forgive or taking action to forgive and more about being receptive to letting go of that which no longer serves us.

Make yourself comfortable and settle in for this meditation on forgiveness. Spend a few minutes following your breath. Just notice it moving into and out of your body. Now, focus your attention on the space between your brows—the low center of your forehead. This is known as your sixth or third eye chakra.

Repeat the word *forgiveness* to yourself as you keep your attention focused on your brow center. Picture the word *forgiveness* and notice the color of the text.

Follow your breath some more and let your body relax. State the following internally or aloud, "*I now let go of my attachment to all that does not serve me. I invite myself to relax into the loving arms of a benevolent universe.*"

Follow your breath some more, and now picture the word *forgiveness* again by focusing on your brow center and saying the word aloud. Notice the color of the text. If it is a dark color, invite it to become a pastel or white color. Do that by talking to it, either in your mind or aloud. You might say something like, "*Dear letters, I invite you to become a lighter, more pastel color, or even white if that would bring you joy.*"

Next, follow your breath a little bit more and then state the following internally or aloud, "*I love, accept, and forgive myself and/or _____ and choose a life of lightness. It is done.*"

Now spend as long as you want in a relaxing meditation following your breath. You can choose to use a mantra if one comes to you. You've set your intention for forgiveness and now, as you meditate in the coming days, weeks, months, and even years, you will be aligning with that intention for your highest good.

## GUIDED MEDITATION FOR SPIRITUAL PROTECTION

Spiritual protection is multifaceted. It means shielding and moderating the endless streams of energy that come at you on a daily basis. You may have heard of the idea of the highly sensitive person shared in the book *The Highly Sensitive Person: How to Thrive When the World Overwhelms You* by Dr. Elaine N. Aron. Many people who are spiritually inclined are highly sensitive simply by virtue of having developed their subtler senses through things like meditation, tai chi, shamanic journeying, and other New Age pursuits. Spiritual protection helps keep you separate from other people's energy, as is needed for your highest good. Think of it like this: Each of us is a plug, and if we plug into every single socket we encounter every second of our lives, our plugs can get fried—it is just too much energy. Putting conscious spiritual protection around you is like a installing a semi-permeable screen; it lets in the positive energy and screens any negative energy.

A spiritual—not religious—being who can be very helpful with spiritual protection is Archangel Michael. This being is dedicated to helping humans feel safe and guiding us to experience happy, positive lives. The invocation of Archangel Michael is useful for protection and feeling extra secure throughout daily life, while sleeping, in crowds, or in challenging situations. Repeat it aloud or internally and feel the atoms surrounding you being infused with Archangel Michael's loving presence. This is great to say before bed, and you may want to post it on your wall or nightstand as a soothing reminder.

Begin by entering a light meditation and following your breath. When you are ready, say the following words out loud:

*"Archangel Michael before me.*
*Archangel Michael behind me.*
*Archangel Michael to the left of me.*
*Archangel Michael to the right of me.*
*Archangel Michael above me.*
*Archangel Michael below me.*
*Archangel Michael is here on Earth.*
*I am love, protected.*
*I am love, protected.*
*I am love, protected.*
*It is done."*

Sit quietly for a few moments, and notice how you feel. Do you feel any sensations in your body? Do you see any color, hear any sounds, or smell any aromas? Do you get a sense of Archangel Michael?

Follow your breath for little bit longer, and when you're ready, return to daily activity.

# GUIDED MEDITATION FOR PROSPERITY

A prosperous life is abundant with everything you could ever need or want: happiness, love, positive relationships, money, fulfillment, creativity, success. When we are prosperous, we are flourishing. We are healthy, happy, safe, and fully supplied with everything we need or desire. When we combine the idea of prosperity with an intention for our highest good and the highest good of all life, we create true wealth.

In this meditation, we will enlist the help of a few deities who are known to help with creating a prosperous life. Demeter is a Greek goddess who was thought to bring an abundant harvest and a prosperous year. Lakshmi is a Hindu goddess of good fortune. These nonphysical beings can help you align with a higher-frequency energy to increase positivity and prosperity in your life through meditation.

Get comfortable, and spend a few minutes following your breath. When you are ready, begin using the following affirmative mantra and meditate, focusing on it for several minutes: *"I gratefully accept the prosperity that easily flows to me every day in every way."*

Next, enlist the help of our prosperity helpers, Demeter and Lakshmi. Say the following aloud: *"I open my heart wide and say yes to a joyful, abundant life. I welcome the presence of Demeter and Lakshmi, and I am grateful for your help. Please help me align with all that is for my highest good. Please help me be open to receiving the abundant prosperity that surrounds me, and continue to amp up the frequency of abundance in my life. Thank you so much."*

Now sit in meditation and follow your breath, and allow yourself to further connect with Demeter and Lakshmi. Make a note of any experiences or insights in your journal. And remember that gratitude is the key to prosperity. You might like to make a commitment to write down at least ten things you are grateful for every night before bed. If you do this for at least twenty-one days, you'll rewire your life in the direction of gratitude and therefore prosperity.

## GUIDED MEDITATION FOR JOY

Meditation in its simplest form can be relatively neutral, which is extremely valuable. That is why it helps us release our attachments. Because it's so neutral, it is not attached to anything—it is simply being present. That is the heart of living mindfully—being completely present in each moment. But one of the amazing gifts that meditation gives us is a relatively clean slate with which we can make a conscious choice to add a certain flavor. What we're doing in these guided meditations is adding in a flavor for our highest good. We do this with the intention to better our lives, because we are also human beings, and the act of living embodies experiencing this world with its ups and downs. While we work at releasing our attachments to the ups and the downs and whether we like them more or less, we still must acknowledge that we are existing in this dualistic world. We are spirits or souls embodying a physical vehicle in a physical world. So why not combine the techniques of living a mindful life with the techniques of living a conscious and intentional life? That is the essence of guided meditation.

Joy is the highest vibration in existence. Joy is a kind of electricity. Imagine it. What would it be like if the electricity that powers your light bulbs was powered with joy? What do you imagine the lighting in the room would be like? This next meditation helps us integrate the energy of joy into our bodies.

Begin by following your breath and getting comfortable for a few minutes. This meditation is best done lying down.

Visualize a ball of golden light before you. Say the word *yes* aloud to this ball three times, and tell the ball that it is joy, also three times.

Ask this ball to expand and encompass the entire room you are in and, if you would like, your entire house and yard. You can do this wherever you are, even in a local coffee shop.

Place your attention on your physical body. Feel every nerve, from the tips of your fingers and toes to your joints and the top of your head. Feel your whole physical body pulsing. Notice its shape.

Call forth ultimate power by saying aloud, "*I call forth all of the magnetic resonance particles in the universe that love joy! Woo-hoo! I am about to throw the best joy party you have ever seen. Please help me. This party is in my [area selected]. Everyone meet there in five . . . four . . . three . . . two . . . one!*"

Clap your hands together vigorously three times (creating a paradigm shift). See and feel the entirety of the joy ball condense into your physical body, completely filling it.

Now, sing or hum aloud. Make up the most joyful songs and sounds. Allow these to spontaneously bubble out of you. If that isn't quite happening, then fake it till you make it.

When you have sang and sounded your heart out, then wind it down a bit vocally, but keep the joyful feeling and let it become a peaceful joy. Feel the joy particles inside of you begin to sway in unison, as if they were holding hands by candlelight in peaceful communion, humming for peace, honoring joy.

If you can, rest for at least thirty minutes and feel yourself in the center of a multitiered circle of the humming, swaying particles. Drift off to sleep if you can.

You will feel when the meditation is complete. The joy and healing will remain for all time.

Use this process as often as you would like and always allow the rest period after for the best results.

## GUIDED MEDITATION FOR LETTING GO OF DENSITY

Throughout the course of our lives, we may experience ups and downs. There will likely be disappointments, and there will be joys. Ideally, we are able to have these experiences and let them pass through us without attaching to them. But we are humans living in duality, and we are wired to attach. The biochemicals in our bodies and the way that our human brains function with those chemicals mean we are literally wired to attach, whether or not we feel something is positive or negative.

Sometimes when something is negative, we get attached to some aspect of the experience or energy involved and store it in the body as a density. Density is simply a pocket of denser energy. Ideally, we want our energy to be highly vibrational and full of light. Densities can bring us down. High vibration can bring us up and help us feel joyful and fulfilled.

In this guided meditation, we will let go of density. We will put down some of our heavy energetic baggage. The Hindu deity Ganesha is known as a remover of obstacles and is the perfect being to help us let go of our density.

Get comfortable, and follow your breath for a few minutes. Next, bring your awareness to the center of your abdomen, just below your bellybutton. You can place one hand over that area. Lots of people carry density in that spot. And consuming alcohol can draw density to your second chakra, which is located right there.

Breathe into your navel area. Let your mind become quiet.

Say the following internally or aloud: "*I allow any density in my body to easily drop out of my energetic field and down into the Earth right now. I thank the Earth for recycling any density that I release back into pure-white light.*"

Follow your breath for a few more minutes as you notice any sensations and how they feel.

When you're ready, state the following aloud: "*I call on Ganesha, remover of obstacles, to help me clear any density from my body and fill me with white light. I also welcome Ganesha's help with anything else that is for my highest good. Please help me elevate my life.*"

Visualize an endless stream of pure-white light like a faucet above you, raining down over you and through you. This stream of white light encompasses all around you in a three-foot radius. The white light flows through you and into you, through every cell of your body. It washes through you. This faucet is pumping white light down through your body, rinsing you out and simultaneously filling you with white light. This faucet is an endlessly supplied source of white light. It can run forever.

When that feels complete, follow your breath for a few minutes and then bring your awareness back into the room. Jot down anything you notice in your journal.

## GUIDED MEDITATION TO OPEN YOUR HEART

When discussing the idea of the "inner witness"—the eternally calm, infinite part of yourself—you might not suspect that the next logical step is a conversation about having an open heart. The inner witness is in fact a big part of having an expansive and open emotional center. In meditation, that's the meaning behind the saying "an open heart." Having an open heart obviously means not closing your heart, and that sounds easy, right? Well, it's actually pretty challenging to maintain.

Every day, we have experiences that might lead us to close our hearts. We feel self-conscious, or we doubt ourselves. Somebody gets mad at us, or we get mad at ourselves because of a decision we made. We are human, and, by definition, that means we are not perfect. We are unique, quirky, and have weaknesses and strengths. And we're diverse. The situation that hurts my feelings and makes me feel like crying might make someone else really mad and want to get in a fistfight, and even another person might not even be affected by it. As a race of human beings, our diversity can be our strength.

We can all find spiritual growth and fulfillment and ultimately experience less suffering in the endeavor to keep an open heart. Our emotional bodies are like a field of constantly moving and flowing energy. The energy moves around and through the body and is anchored at the center of the chest, which some people call the heart chakra. It is one of the main emotional centers. This is a place where emotional energy flows in and out of the body.

When we feel hurt or slighted, that area sometimes constricts. But what if we are able to keep it open and expansive all the time? In the book *The Untethered Soul: The Journey Beyond Yourself*, Michael A. Singer talks about the concept of "samskaras." Samskaras are the impressions of stored energy that are left when we close the heart instead of keeping it open. If we allow an experience—good or bad— to just pass through the body instead of grasping at it or having an aversion to it, which closes the heart, and instead keep the heart open, then we do not create a samskara.

Let's practice!

Sit or lay down somewhere comfortable, where you will be undisturbed for about fifteen or twenty minutes. Find a relaxed posture and follow your breath for a few minutes. Let your mind calm down.

Now bring your attention to the center of your chest. Notice what it feels like. Does it already feel open and expansive? Does it feel partially constricted? You can bring your hands up to massage the area physically; use a dragging motion across the skin, as if you are pulling your hands to the side and opening your chest. Envision opening, relaxing, and expanding and think about the feeling of love. If you would like to use an essential oil, you can mix a rose essential oil with a carrier oil, then rub a small amount into the area and inhale the aroma. (Please make sure to apply the oil on a small patch of skin to test for any adverse reactions before liberally applying.)

If your heart center feels especially constricted, you can use eucalyptus oil (mixed with a carrier oil). This will bring invigorating energy to the area. Sometimes when the area has been constricted for too long, it becomes lethargic or shuts down. In that case, we need to wake it up, but gently, so as not to shake free too many samskaras at once. Ideally, you just want to engage in a gentle process of heart healing that will only enhance your life and not disrupt it. Take your time. There's no rush.

In your relaxed position, keep breathing. Breathe into the center of your chest and really feel it expand on the inhale. Anything that is not love or light will be easily exhaled and released. Breathe more and more deeply each time. As you reach a relaxed state, close your eyes and continue breathing. Let yourself surrender to the sensation. Simply stay open. Let any positive or negative emotions, memories, colors, sounds, or sensations pass through you. Don't grasp at them or attempt to observe them as they pass.

Engage in this heart breathing for as long as you'd like. You can continue to massage your chest as needed. Keep opening and relaxing your heart. Relax your neck. Relax your shoulders, arms, and hands, feeling the heart-based relaxation ripple through your body.

When it feels complete, you can slowly bring your attention back into the room. Vigorously rub your arms and legs. Make sure you feel fully present to yourself. You can state the words "I am here" over and over if you so please.

After you complete this exercise, it's a great idea to drink clean water with a tiny pinch of unprocessed Himalayan or Hawaiian salt. Celtic sea salt also works wonderfully. This helps flush out any toxins that were released during the meditation. When you get rid of emotional toxicity, the body responds by releasing physical toxicity from storage zones in fat cells in the body. So it's important to flush it out.

I also advise that you engage in some vigorous physical exercise after this. If you only have a few minutes, do a set of thirty jumping jacks, or anything that will help you break a sweat and start moving energy. When you meditate to open your heart and clear it, you also engage in powerful physical detoxification.

# GUIDED MEDITATION FOR A COMPASSIONATE LIFE

I believe that compassion is the key to our evolution as a species. By placing attention on what it is like to walk in another's shoes, we step outside of ourselves and into a never-ending community. The current world population is over seven billion and growing rapidly. To accommodate all of these beings, we need a new model for living, and I believe that model is centered in compassion. If we meditate upon this new model of compassion, we can embody it. In the process of becoming conscious beings, we eventually come back around again and again to the ideas of compassion, caring, and empathy.

In this guided meditation, I will introduce you to a powerful and benevolent nonphysical being who can help us connect with the energy of compassion in a deeper way. Her name is Quan Yin (also Kwan Yin or Guan Yin). She is a Buddhist goddess of mercy, and throughout history and mythology, she has been a part of many stories. For this guided meditation, she will join us as a nonphysical being who cares for and loves all of humanity. She offers her assistance to find the deep seeds of compassion within us and help them blossom forth into a bud that will ultimately open into petals of light and bestow blessings upon all we meet.

Sit back and relax, and begin to follow your breath. Make sure you feel comfortable. If you have any rose quartz around, you can hold it or have it nearby. If you have any pale pink clothing, you could wear it, or if you own a pale pink blanket or pillow, you might like to sit with it. That will be the color of focus for this compassion meditation.

Spend a few minutes following your breath. Just allow yourself to relax more and more deeply. When you're ready, place the tip of your tongue against the roof of your mouth right behind your two front teeth. This gesture unifies the two hemispheres of the brain and maximizes your cognitive potential for that moment.

As you sit with your tongue behind your front teeth, focus your attention from your brow center. Visualize a pale pink light coming out from your brain, washing the area in front of you in a pale pink light. Imagine that you're looking at a sheet of fluid and endless light, and focus on the center point of that sheet, right in front of you.

Remove your tongue from the spot behind your teeth and repeat the following mantra quietly in your mind: *Om Mani Padme Hum.* This mantra means hail to the jewel amid the lotus. It is symbolic of the jewel of compassion within your heart center and is used to call the blessings of Quan Yin for yourself and the world.

Repeat the mantra and focus on the pale pink color. Allow yourself to experience deep relaxation and a feeling of opening. When you choose compassion, you feel the interconnection of all life in the universe. And when you invite Quan Yin into your life, doors open and things always improve. Quan Yin also helps us with spontaneous acts of shedding the illusion of duality and the illusion of karma so that we may step out of the repetitive cycle of incarnation and into conscious choice.

As you repeat the mantra, feel Quan Yin stand before you. You can hold out your hands, palms facing up, and, by nodding your head, invite her to hover her spirit hands over your physical hands. You can stop repeating the mantra and allow yourself to simply focus on the sensation of her spirit hands hovering above your physical hands. Feel the exchange of energy. You can introduce yourself and say, *"Hello, my name is . . ."* Listen for a response. It may arrive as pulsing in your hands or a tingling sensation of hot or cold. You may smell or feel something. You may see a color or image. You may hear a tinkling of bells. Or you may simply know that she is there.

Ask any questions you have or for help with anything. And then ask her if there's anything with which you can help her. Sit in communion and communication for as long as you would like. Thank Quan Yin for her presence and guidance.

When the meditation feels complete, you will feel her step back, or if it becomes too overwhelming or you become fatigued, you can say, *"Thank you so much. Let's continue this later."* Feel her step back. Then say aloud, *"I now disconnect from Quan Yin and everyone involved in this meditation as needed for my highest good. I am sealed and protected in all dimensions, all inter-dimensions, and all realities as needed for my highest good."*

When you open your eyes, take a few moments to reconnect to your surroundings. Drink plenty of water. Clap your hands, stomp your feet, and do things to make sure you are feeling present in your body before you go about your day.

# GUIDED MEDITATION FOR BEING PRESENT TO YOUR SENSES

So how can you feel truly present? This question is asked by people from all walks of life, of every age, and in all kinds of ways, like "How can I feel more alive?"

Start simple. With the palms of your hands, start at the soles of your feet and rub briskly, moving up your legs and body, and repeat aloud or in your mind, *"I am here now. I am present."* And just feel what it is like to be fully in your body. Really bring your awareness to that experience.

Now try to bring your conscious awareness to your feet—really inhabit them. Do the same with your feet and legs. Be present in your feet and up through your torso, bringing your awareness all the way to the tips of your fingers. Continue this awareness, bringing it from your feet all the way to the top of your head and throughout your entire body. Can you feel your entire body simultaneously? You might feel this awareness like a pulsing or a tingling.

Consider what might happen if you got into that deeply present place and then explored the sensual aspect of it, whether solo or with a loving partner in the same state of awareness. Would everything be richer and more intense? Would you experience sensations and pleasure in a new way? Would your soul feel fed to know that you are seeing your sacredness and, if a partner is involved, that he or she is, too? Give it a try and find out!

How would it feel to be present while experiencing glorious sensory pleasure?

In your journal, list at least twenty sensory pleasures. Some ideas are: bubble baths; eating cool and flavorful snow cones; the feel of clean, soft sheets during a midafternoon, sun-drenched cat nap.

When you are finished, say the following affirmation aloud: "*I am a sensual being of light. I am fully present in my body, and I'm full of bliss.*"

Experience at least one of these sensual pleasures per day for the next twenty days. Your life will be so much more pleasurable that you will probably want to make another list and experience even more pleasure to awaken your senses every day. Learn to be aware of the ever-flowing bliss in your heart and soul by being present to your senses.

## GROUNDING MEDITATION FOR HEALTH

Over the years, I have learned to monitor how grounded I am at any given moment. The term grounding refers to how present you are in your physical body and how connected you are to the Earth below your feet. I have noticed that the more grounded and connected to the Earth I am, the better I feel physically and emotionally. If I am feeling well-grounded, my mind feels clearer and less cluttered and I view my life as manageable and positive. When I am not feeling well-grounded, it is harder to concentrate and I feel spacey and not present to the moment. It is important to be well-grounded so that you are able to fully integrate what you learn into your physical body, where it can enhance your health.

Grounding is enhanced by being outside and in physical contact with the Earth. You can do this by gardening, walking on the beach with bare feet, hiking through the woods, raking leaves, shoveling snow, resting under a tree and taking a nap, or even breathing in the cool morning air on your porch before starting your day. Get outside; eat foods that are healthful and primarily alive (plants that are raw or lightly cooked, including nuts, brown rice, grains, etc.); drink lots of water—all drinking water has been inside of the Earth at some point; and get plenty of exercise and outdoor activity. Taking slow, deep, cleansing breaths can also help you feel more present and grounded.

Being well-grounded is completely, totally being present to the moment. The present moment, right now, is all that exists. No past, no present, no future; just now. A big part of grounding is being in the now.

Use the following meditation process frequently to help you get in touch with the roots that tether you to the planet, nourish you, and sustain you. Sit or lie down for this exercise. You may do this indoors or outdoors in a safe, quiet space.

Place your attention on the soles of your feet.

Envision roots growing out of each foot and out of your tailbone; visualize sending them into the Earth. They may combine into one large root or remain as three separate roots. Feel these root(s) growing

guided visualization meditations          103

deeper and deeper, through soil and dirt, through the matrix of rock and stone, through aquifers full of water.

Continue growing your root(s) down through the magma and into the mantle of the planet.

Finally, grow your root(s) into the core of the Earth. Feel them be sucked into the inner core of the planet. There they are held. Stable. Strong. Rooted.

Feel the energy and vibration of the Earth flowing up through your root(s) and into your feet and tailbone. Feel it pulsing within you. Hear the inner heartbeat of the planet. Hear it beating like a gentle drum. Merge with this interdimensional sound. Experience deep communion with the Earth. Feel her love for you expand into each cell in your body. All is right with you and your mother, the Earth. She has infinite strength, and she shares this wellspring of stability and strength with you, her child.

Thank the Earth for this huge gift.

Slowly allow your awareness to come back into the room or area in which you are sitting or lying. Feel whatever your body is touching—the chair, the bed, the ground. Wiggle your toes and fingers.

With your awareness fully in the moment and eyes open, feel your root(s) pulsing below you. Maintain this awareness for as long as you are able. Walk around, still feeling your roots. Place your attention on the soles of your feet. Experience what it feels like to be fully present and grounded in the moment, in the now.

# CONCLUSION

I hope you have enjoyed this journey through the art and science of meditation! Remember there is a quiet, gentle witness inside of you lovingly watching everything you do and simply being present to your magnificence. You are a soul and spirit incarnated in a physical form, and there are myriad tools available to you to ease the journey and make it worthwhile. Meditation is one of those great tools. Use it.

# ACKNOWLEDGMENTS

Thank you to Lisa Hagan for believing in my message and my work and for being such an incredible support and blessing in my life. Thank you to Kate Zimmermann for being the impetus to bring this book into the world and for shaping it into the work it is today. Thank you to Stephanie Rutt for sharing the experience of abdominal breathing with me in a yoga class back in the late '90s. Obviously it really stuck with me! Thank you to all the helpful spirits and beings, physical and nonphysical, who have made this book possible and have allowed me to do the work that I love. Thank you to my ever-loving and wonderful family and friends.

# ABOUT THE AUTHOR

Amy Leigh Mercree's motto is "Live joy. Be kind. Love unconditionally." She counsels women and men in the underrated art of self-love to create happier lives. Mercree is a bestselling author, media personality, and medical intuitive. She speaks internationally, focusing on kindness, joy, and wellness.

Mercree is the bestselling author of *The Spiritual Girl's Guide to Dating: Your Enlightened Path to Love, Sex, and Soul Mates*; *A Little Bit of Chakras: An Introduction to Energy Healing*; *Joyful Living: 101 Ways to Transform Your Spirit and Revitalize Your Life*; *The Chakras and Crystals Cookbook: Juices, Sorbets, Smoothies, Salads, and Crystal Infusions to Empower Your Energy Centers*; and *The Compassion Revolution: 30 Days of Living from the Heart*.

Mercree has been featured in *Glamour*, Huffington Post, *Aspire*, YourTango, *Spirituality & Health*, *LA Yoga*, *Latina*, *Soul & Spirit*, *Women's Health*, and *Inc.*

Check out AmyLeighMercree.com for articles and quizzes. Mercree is fast becoming one of the most quoted women on the Web. See what all the buzz is about @AmyLeighMercree on Twitter, Snapchat, and Instagram.

To download your FREE meditation toolkit and get your Zen on right now, go to www.amyleighmercree.com/meditationtoolkit—password MEDITATION.

# BIBLIOGRAPHY

"A Beginner's Guide To Chakra Meditation." *Mindvalley Academy Blog.* Accessed Dec. 8, 2016. http://bit.ly/2opFs41.

"All-Embracing Compassion-The Heart-Practice of Tonglen." *Metta Refuge.* Accessed Dec. 8, 2016. http://bit.ly/2opEg0w.

Alpert, Yelena Moroz. "13 Major Yoga Mantras to Memorize." *Yoga Journal.* Feb. 25, 2016. http://bit.ly/1VNuCQJ.

Ancient Yoga. "The Mudra of Life | Strengthen Immunity with the Prana Mudra." YouTube video. 6:39. Sept. 13, 2016. http://bit.ly/2pORwgr.

"An Interview with Llewellyn Vaughan-Leefrom the Sounds True Catalogue—Summer 1998." *The Golden Sufi Center.* Accessed Dec. 7, 2016. http://bit.ly/2pOVQMR.

Aron, Elaine N. *The Highly Sensitive Person: How to Thrive When the World Overwhelms You.* New York, NY: First Broadway Books, 1998.

Atkins, Shira. "A Beginner's Guide to Essential Sanskrit Mantras." *Sonima.* Aug. 21, 2015. http://bit.ly/1MX8WiU.

"AUM Chanting for the Thirsty." *Isha.* Oct. 3, 2012. http://bit.ly/2p1Gm8d.

"Awakened Heart Project for Jewish Meditation and Contemplative Judaism." *Awakened Heart Project for Contemplative Judaism.* Accessed Dec. 7, 2016. http://bit.ly/2pe34xu.

Axel, Gabriel. "Your Brain on Om: The Science of Mantra." *U.S. News.* Oct. 2, 2013. http://bit.ly/1ox0B9A.

Barenblat, Rachel. "A short history of Jewish meditation." *Velveteen Rabbi.* Feb. 10, 2014. http://bit.ly/2peaJfc.

Barnes, Vernon A., et al. "Impact of Transcendental Meditation on Psychotropic Medication Use Among Active Duty Military Service Members With Anxiety and PTSD." *Military Medicine* 181, vol. 1 (2016): 56–63. doi: 10.7205/MILMED-D-14-00333.

Berkers, Ewald. "Opening the Chakras." *Eclectic Energies*. Accessed Dec. 8, 2016. http://bit.ly/29S8l69.

Black, David S., and George M. Slavich. "Mindfulness Meditation and the Immune System: A Systematic Review of Randomized Controlled Trials." *Annals of the New York Academy of Sciences* 1373, no. 1 (2016): 13–24. doi: 10.1111/nyas.12998.

Bogdani, Pravit. *Chakra Meditation: A User-Friendly Guide to Opening, Balancing, and Cleansing through Chakra Meditation Techniques.* Amazon CreateSpace, 2015.

"Brief History of Qigong." *Institute of Qigong & Integrative Medicine*. Accessed Dec. 8, 2016. http://bit.ly/2pORxBc.

Bullitt, John. "What is Theraveda Buddhism?" *Buddhist Studies: Buddha Dharma Association & BuddhaNet*. Accessed Feb. 21, 2017. http://bit.ly/2oRZlVt.

Burstein, Mandy. "5 Ancient Mantras That Will Transform Your Life." *Mindybodygreen*. Mar. 22, 2013. http://bit.ly/1bhTMF9.

Carter, Christine. "Greater Happiness in 5 Minutes a Day." *Greater Good Science Center*. Sept. 10, 2012. http://bit.ly/1wT50KC.

Carver, Leo. "10 Powerful Mudras and How to Use Them." *The Chopra Center*. Accessed Apr. 18, 2017. http://bit.ly/2nb5Nmz.

Catlett, Matthew. "21 Mantras for Meditation." *Programming Life*. Dec. 21, 2015. http://bit.ly/2oJxchi.

Cianciosi, John. "Use Mindful Nature Walks To Deepen Your Meditation Practice." *Yoga Journal*. Aug. 28, 2007. http://bit.ly/2oQEQK7.

Clarke, Tainya C., et al. "Trends in the Use of Complementary Health Approaches Among Adults: United States, 2002–2012." *National Health Statistics Reports* 79 (2015). http://bit.ly/1DCXGD8.

*Contemplative Literature: A Comparative Sourcebook on Meditation and Contemplative Prayer*. Edited by Komjathy. Albany, NY: State University of New York Press, 2015.

Cooper, David A. *The Handbook of Jewish Meditation Practices: A Guide for Enriching the Sabbath and Other Days of Your Life.* Woodstock, VT: Jewish Lights Publishing, 2000.

"Current World Population." *Worldometers.* Accessed May 30, 2017. http://bit.ly/Ism9T6.

Desbordes, Gaëlle, et al. "Effects of Mindful-attention and Compassion Meditation Training on Amygdala Response to Emotional Stimuli in an Ordinary, Non-meditative State." *Frontiers in Human Neuroscience* 6, no. 292 (2012). doi: 10.3389/fnhum.2012.00292.

Dianda, Don. "The Opening of the American Psyche: A Brief History of Zen in the West." *Elephant Journal.* Nov. 6, 2012. http://bit.ly/2nWka2O.

Dubov, Nissan Dovid. "Jewish Meditation." *Chabad.org.* Accessed Apr. 18, 2017. http://bit.ly/2pwgp42.

Editors of Encyclopædia Britannica. "Om: Indian Religion." *Encyclopædia Britannica.* Last updated May 1, 2015. http://bit.ly/2nZVvKC.

Fondin, Michelle. "What Is A Chakra?" *The Chopra Center.* Accessed Dec. 8, 2016. http://bit.ly/2pPfkka.

Fox, K. C., et al. "Is Meditation Associated with Altered Brain Structure? A Systematic Review and Meta-analysis of Morphometric Neuroimaging in Meditation Practitioners." *Neuroscience & Biobehavioral Reviews* 43 (2014): 48-73. doi: 10.1016/j.neubiorev.2014.03.016.

Frawley, David. "Vedantic Meditation." *SwamiJ.* Accessed Dec. 6, 2016. http://bit.ly/2pwa0Wp.

Geethanjali - Yoga. "Yoga Hand Mudras - Top 5 Mudras for Good Health and Weight Loss - Benefits." Youtube video. 8:28. Jul. 21, 2015. http://bit.ly/2oRZ9pm.

Goyal, Madhav, et al. "Meditation Programs for Psychological Stress and Well-being." *JAMA Internal Medicine* 174, no. 3 (2014): 357. doi: 10.1001/jamainternmed.2013.13018.

"Guidelines for Walking a Labyrinth." *Sacredwalk*. Accessed Dec. 8, 2016. http://bit.ly/2nZEwIh.

Heckert, Lynne. "An Overview of Buddhist Meditation." *Philadelphia Meditation*. Accessed Dec. 06, 2016. http://bit.ly/2prOBOe.

Heller, Rick. *Secular Meditation: 32 Practices for Cultivating Inner Peace, Compassion, and Joy—A Guide from the Humanist Community at Harvard*. Novato, CA: New World Library, 2015.

Hirschi, Gertrud. *Mudras: Yoga in Your Hands: A Simple Technique to Achieve Lasting Health, Happiness, and Inner Peace*. Newburyport, MA: Red Wheel/Weiser Books, 2000.

Hwang, Yoon-Suk, et al. "Cultivating Mind: Mindfulness Interventions for Children with Autism Spectrum Disorder and Problem Behaviours, and Their Mothers." *Journal of Child and Family Studies* 24, no.10 (2015): 3093–3106. doi: 10.1007/s10826-015-0114-x.

*Institute for Jewish Spirituality*. Accessed Dec. 7, 2016. http://www. jewishspirituality.org/.

Inzitari, D., et al. "White Matter Changes: The Clinical Consequences in the Aging Population." *Journal of Neural Transmission* 59 (2000): 1–8. http://bit.ly/2opFLMs.

Jabr, Ferris. "Self-Awareness with a Simple Brain." *Scientific American*. Nov. 1, 2012. http://bit.ly/2nZ5hwE.

Kadden, Bruce, and Barbara Binder Kadden. *Teaching Tefilah: Insights and Activities on Prayer*. Denver, CO: A.R.E. Publications, 2004.

Koike, Marcia Kiyomi, and Roberto Cardoso. "Meditation Can Produce Beneficial Effects to Prevent Cardiovascular Disease." *Hormone Molecular Biology and Clinical Investigation* 18, no. 3 (2014): 137–143. doi: 10.1515/hmbci-2013-0056.

Kumar, Sanjay, et al. "Meditation on *OM*: Relevance from Ancient Texts and Contemporary Science." *International Journal of Yoga* 3, no. 1 (2010): 2–5. doi: 10.4103/0973-6131.66771.

la Cour, Peter, and Marian Petersen. 2015. "Effects of Mindfulness Meditation on Chronic Pain: A Randomized Controlled Trial." *Pain Medicine* 16, no. 4 (2014): 641–652. DOI: 10.1111/pme.12605.

Laneri, Davide, et al. "Effects of Long-Term Mindfulness Meditation on Brain's White Matter Microstructure and Its Aging." *Frontiers in Aging Neuroscience* 7 (2016): 254. doi:10.3389/fnagi.2015.00254.

"Learn Transcendental Meditation." *The Meditation Trust.* Accessed Dec. 8, 2016. http://bit.ly/2pdVLG6.

Lew, Alan. "Prayer and the Uses of Meditation." *Judaism: A Quarterly Journal of Life and Thought* 49, no. 1 (2000): 93–101. http://bit.ly/2nZHgW7.

Lewis, Mark. "New Age Meditation." *Project-Meditation.* Accessed Apr. 18, 2017. http://bit.ly/2oka5Jg.

Malinowski, Peter. "Neural Mechanisms of Attentional Control in Mindfulness Meditation." *Frontiers in Neuroscience* 7, vol. 8 (2013). doi: 10.3389/fnins.2013.00008.

"Manifesting True Success." *Chopra Center Meditation.* Accessed Apr. 18, 2017. http://bit.ly/2okiaNP.

Mayo Clinic Staff. "Chronic Stress Puts Your Health at Risk." *Mayo Clinic.* Apr. 16, 2016. http://mayocl.in/1aOXhUi.

McEwen, Bruce S., and Peter J. Gianaros. "Central Role of the Brain in Stress and Adaptation: Links to Socioeconomic Status, Health, and Disease." *Annals of the New York Academy of Sciences* 1186 (2010): 190–222. doi: 10.1111/j.1749-6632.2009.05331.x.

"Medical Definition of Neuroplasticity." *MedicineNet.* Accessed Nov. 16, 2016. http://bit.ly/1ZMWaY8.

"Meditation: In Depth." *National Center for Complementary and Integrative Health.* Last updated Apr. 2016. http://bit.ly/1BQ4I9l.

Muse, Azuka. "The Best Mudras and Yoga Asanas for Women's Health." *Parimukti Yoga and Meditation India.* Dec. 16, 2015. http://bit.ly/2nZVQgo.

Myss, Caroline. "Sufism in the U.S.A." *Caroline Myss*. Accessed Dec. 8, 2016. http://bit.ly/2nWnCKE.

Ñānadhammo, Ajahn. "Three Expositions on Walking Meditation." In "Walking Meditation." *The Wheel Publication* 464 (2007): 6–27. http://bit.ly/2oQFjfm.

"Nationwide survey reveals widespread use of mind and body practices." *National Institutes of Health*. Feb. 10, 2015. http://bit.ly/2oYz4Bi.

"'Om Mani Padme Hum': 'Hail to the Jewel Lotus.'" *Sacred Wind*. Accessed May 30, 2017. http://bit.ly/2qxFZ5R.

Ong, Jason C., et al. "A Randomized Controlled Trial of Mindfulness Meditation for Chronic Insomnia." *Sleep* 37, no. 9 (2014): 1553–1563. doi: 10.5665/sleep.4010.

Puff, Robert. "An Overview of Meditation: Its Origins and Traditions." *Psychology Today*. Jul. 7, 2013. http://bit.ly/1MoOuY4.

Rees, Brian, et al. "Significant Reductions in Posttraumatic Stress Symptoms in Congolese Refugees Within 10 days of Transcendental Meditation Practice." *Journal of Traumatic Stress* 27, no. 1 (2014): 112–115. doi: 10.1002/jts.21883.

"Religions: Meditation." *BBC*. Last updated Nov. 24, 2009. http://bbc.in/2oniZot.

Singer, Michael A. *The Untethered Soul: The Journey Beyond Yourself*. Oakland, CA: New Harbinger Publications, 2007.

Shyamalila. "Sanskrit Mantras." *EnkiVillage*. Accessed Apr. 18, 2017. http://bit.ly/2opER2g.

Slagter, Heleen A., et al. "Mental Training Affects Distribution of Limited Brain Resources." *PLOS Biology* 5, no. 6 (2007). doi: 10.1371/journal.pbio.0050138.

Smith, Huston, and Philip Novak. *Buddhism: A Concise Introduction*. New York: HarperCollins Publishers, 2003.

Tang, Yi-Yuan, et al. "The Neuroscience of Mindfulness Meditation." *Nature Reviews Neuroscience* 16 (2015): 213–225. doi: 10.1038/nrn3916.

"The Benefits of AUM Chanting" in "Mantras Explained: How a Mantra Can Lead to Transformation." *Isha*. Jan. 27, 2015. http://bit.ly/2oRZico.

"The Legend of Quan Yin: Goddess of Mercy." *Holy Mountain Trading Company*. Accessed May 30, 2017. http://bit.ly/2rRKRGW.

Trungpa, Chögyam. *Training the Mind and Loving-Kindness Meditation*. Boston, MA: Shambhala Publications, 2003.

"Types of Prayer." *Prayer Eleven: School of Christian Prayer*. Accessed May 30, 2017. http://bit.ly/2rgk7x0.

"Use of Complementary Health Approaches in the U.S." *National Center for Complementary and Integrative Health*. Last updated Aug. 10, 2016. http://bit.ly/1CEmvNI.

V, Jayaram. "Dhyana or Meditation in Hindu Tradition." *Hindu Website*. Accessed Dec. 7, 2016. http://bit.ly/1dUpgiG.

Vaughan-Lee, Llewellyn. "The Sufi Meditation of the Heart." In *The Experience of Meditation*. Edited by Jonathan Shear. *The Golden Sufi Center*. Accessed Dec. 6, 2016. https://goldensufi.org/a_meditation_of_heart.html.

Veylanswami, Satguru Bodhinatha. "YOGA: A Youthful Primer About Hinduism's Eight-Limbed System of Meditation and Spiritual Striving." *Hinduism Today* 32, no. 1 (Jan–Mar 2010): 37–53.. http://bit.ly/2oPRMyH.

Waters, Lea, et al. "Contemplative Education: A Systematic, Evidence-Based Review of the Effect of Meditation Interventions in Schools." *Educational Psychology Review* 27, no. 1 (2015): 103–134. doi: 10.1007/s10648-014-9258-2.

"Welcome to ScienceOfMudra.com." *Harisingh*. Accessed Apr. 18, 2017. http://bit.ly/1HvZFg7.

"What Bahá'ís Believe: The Life of the Spirit." *Bahai.org*. Accessed May 1, 2017. http://bit.ly/2oYunHB.

"What is Meditation." *The World Community for Christian Meditation*. Accessed Apr. 18, 2017. http://bit.ly/1nMd2km.

Wieczner, Jen. "Meditation Has Become A Billion-Dollar Business." *Fortune*. March 12, 2016. http://for.tn/1QVBhVq.

Willoughby, Deborah. "Mantra Meditation in Early Christianity." *Yoga International*. May 14, 2013. http://bit.ly/2nWjnPa.

Wilson, Jeff. *Mindful America: The Mutual Transformation of Buddhist Meditation and American Culture*. New York: Oxford University Press, 2014.

Yoshimura, Mitsunobu, et al. "Disaster Relief for the Japanese Earthquake-Tsunami of 2011: Stress Reduction Through the Transcendental Meditation® Technique." *Psychological Reports* 117, no. 1 (2015): 206–216. doi: 10.2466/02.13.PR0.117c11z6.

# INDEX